WITHDRAWN

THE DISTORTION
OF AMERICA

also by Oscar Handlin

BOSTON'S IMMIGRANTS: A STUDY IN ACCULTURATION (1941)

THIS WAS AMERICA (1949)

THE UPROOTED (1951; second edition, enlarged, 1973)

ADVENTURE IN FREEDOM (1954)

HARVARD GUIDE TO AMERICAN HISTORY (1954)

AMERICAN PEOPLE IN THE TWENTIETH CENTURY (1954)

CHANCE OR DESTINY (1955)

RACE AND NATIONALITY IN AMERICAN LIFE (1957)

READINGS IN AMERICAN HISTORY (1957)

AL SMITH AND HIS AMERICA (1958)

IMMIGRATION AS A FACTOR IN AMERICAN HISTORY (1959)

JOHN DEWEY'S CHALLENGE TO AMERICAN EDUCATION (1959)

THE NEWCOMERS: NEGROES AND PUERTO RICANS IN A CHANGING
METROPOLIS (1959)

AMERICAN PRINCIPLES AND ISSUES: THE NATIONAL PURPOSE (1961)

THE AMERICANS (1963)

FIRE-BELL IN THE NIGHT: THE CRISIS IN CIVIL RIGHTS (1964)

CHILDREN OF THE UPROOTED (1966)

STATUE OF LIBERTY (1971)

PICTORIAL HISTORY OF IMMIGRATION (1972)

OCCASIONS FOR LOVE (1977)

TRUTH IN HISTORY (1979)

with Mary F. Handlin

COMMONWEALTH: A STUDY OF THE ROLE OF GOVERNMENT
IN AMERICAN ECONOMY (1947)

DIMENSIONS OF LIBERTY (1961)

POPULAR SOURCES OF POLITICAL AUTHORITY (1966)

THE AMERICAN COLLEGE AND AMERICAN CULTURE (1970)

FACING LIFE: YOUTH AND THE FAMILY IN AMERICAN HISTORY (1971)

THE WEALTH OF THE AMERICAN PEOPLE (1975)

with Lilian Handlin

ABRAHAM LINCOLN AND THE UNION (1980)

Oscar Handlin

THE DISTORTION OF AMERICA

An Atlantic Monthly Press Book

Little, Brown and Company — Boston–Toronto

FIRST EDITION

LIBRARY OF CONGRESS CATALOGING IN PUBLICATION DATA

Handlin, Oscar, 1915–
    The distortion of America.

    "An Atlantic Monthly Press book."
    1. United States — Foreign relations — 1945–
    2. United States — Foreign relations — 1933–1945.
    I. Title
    E744.H348   327.73   81-4346
    ISBN 0-316-34316-1   AACR2

ATLANTIC–LITTLE, BROWN BOOKS
ARE PUBLISHED BY
LITTLE, BROWN AND COMPANY
IN ASSOCIATION WITH
THE ATLANTIC MONTHLY PRESS

BP
Designed by Susan Windheim
Published simultaneously in Canada
by Little, Brown & Company (Canada) Limited

PRINTED IN THE UNITED STATES OF AMERICA

For Sam,
with hope

Contents

Preface

IN 1980 the disarray of American foreign policy raised a painful question: Was the deterioration of the American position as a great power foreseeable?

Something was wrong. And the presidential campaign in the fall of that year shed little light on it. But the evidence pointed to a weakening of United States influence everywhere in the world. Not long before, Iran and the Arabian peninsula were the two pillars of Western security; in October, almost a year had passed while American hostages languished in Tehran and a bitter war put the whole region at hazard. The difficult efforts at détente with the Soviet Union seemed to have come to naught; friends and allies doubted the United States' capabilities and questioned its intentions; and the country had lost many painfully won positions. Most ominous and least noticed, the great powers no longer regarded nuclear war as an unthinkable means of mutual destruction: they shifted strategy and tactics to the thinkable methods of using atomic weapons for limited purposes. The United States seemed unable to defend the national interest, or even to define what the national interest was. A sense of helplessness, of drift, of inability to control events often led to indecision. Regarded from the perspective of the historian, the present formed a striking contrast with the situation thirty years before.

This setting justified a review of my occasional writings over a long period. Now is not the time for a dispassionate history. The evidence is simply not available, and may not be in our lifetime. Though it rests upon the best information at hand, the analysis that follows is polemic and passionate, animated by a sense of urgency and by a commitment to freedom, which is everywhere in danger.

This review calls attention to trends discerned three decades ago, now confirmed by unfolding events. It reveals the disintegration of a once coherent foreign policy that provided the context for decisions on specific issues as they arose. That policy emanated from a clear view of the United States' situation in the world; and it elicited broad popular support. The unraveling of consensus and the loss of perspective necessarily imparted an improvised, ad hoc quality to vital decisions. Hence, the concern over national purpose and the present crisis.

The crisis coincided with a shift in Soviet attitudes that followed upon the failure of Communism. The subsequent realignment of policy and Russia's more aggressive stance were all the more dangerous because of a weakening of commitment to international legality around the world. A paradox resulted: in many countries, neutralism became both more attractive and less tenable. The trend reached its climax in the trauma of Vietnam — a debacle from which the United States has not yet recovered.

The causes of the shift within the United States were both intellectual and social. For reasons connected with their own situation in society, the intellectuals, who should have articulated the country's views, ceased to do so and adopted an adversary posture that contributed to the dual loss of will and sense of purpose. Furthermore, liberalism by its own success destroyed the basis for consensus, without which Americans faced dangerous problems of security. All too often it was easier to evade or postpone problems than to confront them.

Hesitancy, indecision, and uncertainty left too many ambiguities for comfort. In any negotiation where one side did not dictate to another, compromise — give and take — made agreement possible. Where the parties were poles apart, as at Potsdam in 1945 or Geneva in 1954, they could at least agree to disagree and postpone a settlement to later. But in the 1970s, seeming settlements rested upon deliberate misunderstandings. The Paris peace accord of 1973 meant one thing to Le Duc Tho, another to Henry Kissinger; the Senate ratified the Canal treaties with reservations the government of Panama did not accept; the Camp David accords took the form of separate exchanges with Israel and Egypt, along with explanatory codicils, that bore radically different meanings both at the time and later to President Sadat, President Carter, and Prime Minister Begin. Each such pretense left troublesome claims against the future.

Time for a resolution grows short, but may not yet have run out; and perspective from the recent past may help set the issues in their context.

THE DISTORTION
OF AMERICA

1

From Dream to Nightmare

A COHERENT CONCEPT informed American foreign policy for more than a quarter-century. The idea took form just before global war spread to the United States in 1941, and dissolved at some point in the 1960s. In retrospect, the concept of collective security may appear to have been illusory — the desperate dream of desperate people who longed for peace and feared war. Yet now, in the 1980s, deprived of that guide to relations with the outer world, Americans move like figures in a nightmare, locked in a maze with no apparent exit, trapped in a game with every possible outcome dismaying. An era of unlimited promise turned abruptly into one of boundless despair.

No state paper explicitly outlined the policy of collective security. Nor did any diplomat or group of them think its implications through in advance. Rather, the product of historical necessity, it took form in a broad popular consensus when the nation confronted unprecedented obligations inherited from the costly war from which it had just emerged in 1945.

On October 5, 1937, Franklin Delano Roosevelt had recognized the problem but not yet the solution to it. He had until then given little attention to foreign affairs, and if not himself an isolationist, he listened to close advisers who were. Like any reasonable man of his time, he wondered how "any nation could be so foolish and ruthless as to run the risk of plunging the whole world into war by invading" the territory of other nations. Yet, he noted, the actions of Japan in China even then threatened "the peace of the world and the welfare and security of every nation." War, he knew, was a contagion. Declared or undeclared, it could engulf states remote from the original scene of hostilities; and the United States could not insure itself against the dangers of involvement. In the face of an epidemic of physical disease, the community quarantined the patients in order to protect the health of all. Something similar was essential, he argued, if civilization was to survive the epidemic of world lawlessness. The will for peace had to express itself so that countries tempted to violate their agreements and the rights of others would desist. Yet the president proposed no practical program; after the flurry of general statements, he could only appeal to the principles of the Prince of Peace to revive shattered trust among the peoples.

Roosevelt had no clear idea of what he meant. He had come to Chicago to dedicate a Public Works Administration bridge, and unexpectedly spoke about the world situation. The crowd shouted approval, but the strong words shocked Secretary of State Cordell Hull in Washington, and isolationists in Congress began to speak of impeachment. An American Federation of Labor resolution came out against involvement in foreign wars. "It is a terrible thing," Roosevelt later said to a close adviser, "to look over your shoulder when you are trying to lead — and to find no one there." When reporters tried to interpret the Chicago speech, the president was evasive: he had not intended to repudiate neutrality but to expand on it. A few days later he announced that the United States would participate in a conference with Japan and he thus put sanctions out of the question.

United States policy had developed no further when war swept across the world in 1939. The Axis leaders had every reason to believe that the United States would remain passively neutral in the face of their aggressions. But changes in popular attitudes prefigured a broader understanding of the penalties of neutralism, of the need for collective action. As appeasement only enlarged the appetites of the aggressors, Americans began to take heed of the caution in Ernest Hemingway's *For Whom the Bell Tolls* (1940): no man was an island unto himself; the fate of one affected all. No more conclusive evidence was needed than the spectacle of young Frenchmen struggling vainly to hold the Maginot Line in the spring of 1940. Two years earlier they had asked, "Why die for Danzig?"

Though the president was cautious, ever mindful of the need to look over his shoulder, he tried to mold a policy as the fighting spread. War was evil; but perhaps good could come of it, and the greatest good would be an international structure to prevent its recurrence. Roosevelt did not use the old slogan "a war to end war." But he tried to think through the shape of a future peace settlement even before the United States openly joined the contest. He had no desire to repeat Woodrow Wilson's error in becoming a belligerent before getting Allied agreement on objectives. The president and Churchill therefore signed a statement of aims in the Atlantic Charter of August 14, 1941, renouncing any territorial gains; the purpose of the conflict was purely resistance to aggression. On January 1, 1942, in the Declaration of the United Nations, twenty-six of the governments engaged in the war endorsed the Atlantic Charter. The general declaration of October 30, 1943, by the foreign ministers of the United States, Britain, and Russia envisaged the creation of an international organization open to all peace-loving states, "large and small, for the maintenance of international peace and security."

In December of the same year, the inadequacies of those phrases began to show. At a meeting with Roosevelt and Churchill in Tehran, Stalin insisted on annexing the eastern provinces of Poland and proposed to compensate that country with German territory. So much for the renunciation of territorial gains. Furthermore, the Russians would give no assurances about the fate of Eastern Europe at the time when the Soviet Union would be the only military power there.

Roosevelt shied away from the implications of these important unresolved questions and refused to inform the public about them. While the fighting continued he wished to believe that the Big Four were all peace-loving, democratic states, united by common goals. The Office of War Information and many respectable commentators, as well as outright Communist sympathizers, busily disseminated the impression that the Soviet Union was very much like the United States and glossed over the very real differences between them. A great guy, dresses colorfully, likes a stiff drink, smokes a pipe, good sense of humor, simple, childlike — thus Wendell Willkie summed up his impression of Uncle Joe Stalin.

As the end of the war approached, however, the president began to brood about the frightening distance between his views and Stalin's. The Yalta agreements recognized the primacy of Russian influence in Central and Eastern Europe, just as they did Western control in Italy. In practice, however, liberal parties in Eastern Europe enjoyed no such tolerance as the Western powers granted the Communists who entered the French united-front government and those who organized and campaigned openly in Italy. Stalin's promise to broaden the regimes in Poland and Yugoslavia and to permit free elections there and elsewhere proved valueless. The weakness of the Allies lay in their weariness with war and their wishful thinking about Stalin's motives. The strength of the Soviet Union lay in its willingness to go as far as necessary to get what it wished. The Russian people were also tired of war, but they had no voice in forming the judgments of their leaders.

Roosevelt nonetheless tried to persuade himself of the genuineness of face-saving formulas. His hopes turned, as Wilson's had, on creation of an international organization able to rectify any errors in the peace settlement. More than a year of drafting went into the charter of the United Nations formally adopted at the San Francisco conference (June 1945). A General Assembly in which all peace-loving nations each had one vote and a smaller Security Council with power to act would put a brake upon aggression.

For a time wishful thinking fanned life into the hopes acquired at so heavy a cost; and so long as a flicker remained, no one wished to abandon the faith that the war had not all been in vain. Perhaps in time the East European regimes would evolve toward more humane forms. Perhaps the United Nations would fulfill its peace-preserving mission.

Apologists explained away the fate of Czechoslovakia in 1948 and grasped at any sign of improvement. In June 1953 Berlin's mayor, Ernst Reuter, cabled American friends: "Red Empire Crumbles." Strikes had erupted in Pilsen, Czechoslovakia, and riots had spread across East Germany. "Do the men of the Kremlin think they can long rule by means of the bayonet and the tank?" Reuter incredulously asked. The answer was not long in coming. They did think so. And they succeeded. In November 1955 the former general secretary of the Hungarian Trade Union Council predicted that his countrymen would turn out their government in a free election. They did within a year, and even without the miracle of totally free access to the polls. But the Soviet Union also made its will known — with tanks. And it drove the lesson home in Poland; and made it plentifully clear in 1968 in Czechoslovakia. Talk of liberation ebbed in the West except in wisps of wistful speculation about socialism with a human face.

The United Nations Charter remained, with its explicit prohibition of the use of force against the territorial integrity or political independence of any state. But the provision was not self-enforcing. The Soviet Union, like other permanent members, had a veto over the actions of the Security Council and exercised it freely; the General Assembly was a weak and uncertain debating chamber.

The extravagant expectations nurtured by war dropped away after 1949. Eastern Europe sank into uneasy acceptance of satellite status, ruled by surrogates of Russian masters; and the Chinese mainland fell under the sway of an indigenous Communist party. Americans sometimes teased themselves with recriminations, debating whether it need or need not have happened, but few deceived themselves into believing that a reversal of fortunes would soon allow national aspirations, democracy, or the four freedoms to flourish in the lands behind the iron curtain. The United States accepted the Polish, Czech, Hungarian, Rumanian, and Albanian regimes, like them or no; and it prepared to do the same in China.

Of the wartime hopes, there remained only that of peace — that of avoiding a recurrence of open combat, particularly since any war between the great powers might turn atomic and endanger all human survival. And peace hinged on acceptance of the rule of respect for territorial boundaries. Yet, again and again, actions that emanated from the Soviet bloc threatened that sole residue of the wartime aims.

Unhappily, neither of Roosevelt's successors in the fifteen years after his death possessed the gift of language. Truman's speech, direct in ordinary discourse, inadequately expressed his native shrewdness in large matters. Eisenhower, charmingly persuasive in face-to-face encounters, was all but inarticulate in more general communications. Both presidents therefore depended upon intermediaries to put their thoughts into words — most of them men of legal training, accustomed less to considering the merits of the case than to making the winning argument for it. Since in this instance the public was judge and jury, public-relations considerations weighed heavily in the rhetorical formulation of issues.

Unhappily too, PR seemed to dictate a stress upon anti-Communism, particularly after Senator Joseph McCarthy irresponsibly distorted the problem. There had been errors in policy in the 1940s and instances of disloyalty in government; and by pleading the Fifth Amendment rather than defending their views openly, the motley crew of witnesses lent plausibility to suspicions of wrongdoing. But the investigations and hearings shifted attention away from espionage — real and dangerous — to dissent, often that of well-intentioned if misguided members of front organizations.

Tempted by the Red-baiting furor of the early 1950s, speechwriters embellished foreign policy statements with empty anti-Communist declarations calling for the liberation of Eastern Europe and for the unleashing of Chiang Kai-shek. The flow of rhetoric, even from our secretary of state, was an immense, unnecessary, and therefore harmful distraction. No one in the United States government, not least John Foster Dulles, intended to unseat the governments of Poland and Hungary or to urge Chiang to invade the mainland.

American policy followed quite a different course. Intertwined with the anti-Red verbiage was a line adhered to with steadily increasing consistency. The United States accepted the Communist regimes where they existed and made no effort to oust them, in the hope that time would ease the oppression of the subject peoples. But it proposed to help contain the forcible spread of Soviet power by coming to the aid of states under attack — because aggression was a menace not only to the immediate victims but to everyone.

In effect, collective security as Truman and Eisenhower applied it gave life to FDR's vague perception in 1937. Despite all the costs of war and all the hopes of peace, little had survived of the aspiration for a code of international law that would define the rules of conduct among states, other than the insistence that it was not right, whatever the cause, for one nation to launch an armed attack upon another. Such breaches of peace threatened to embroil the whole world in war.

The lead of the United States in atomic weapons through most of this period generated a sense of security about the ability to adhere to that standard. The North Atlantic Treaty Organization (NATO) could offset larger Russian conventional forces and inhibit an attack in Europe, while nuclear superiority deterred adventures elsewhere.

The dangers lay in two sources. The incomplete peace of 1945 left some countries divided, either because the settlement was provisional or because of disputes over issues of sovereignty. And the criterion of a clearly recognized line to cross was unavailing when one country used subversion against another, operating surreptitiously or through intermediaries to bring another state down from within. Fifth-column tactics had been familiar since the 1930s; but free societies still lacked the means to cope with them adequately.

Around the world, failure to complete the peace left unstable areas with uncertain boundaries. The inability to agree upon Germany's future left the occupying powers in place. Zones intended as provisional gradually hardened into a Western and an Eastern state. Here, the determination to resist was so clear that neither side ventured to push hard against the other. The Russians attempted to cut Berlin's communications with the outer world in 1948, but did not dare interfere with the airlift that kept the city supplied. On the other hand, the Americans, while protesting, did not dare act against the wall that illegally cut the eastern sections off from the rest of the city.

Two Chinas appeared — one on Taiwan and one on the mainland. Neither recognized the legitimacy of the other; and occasional exchanges of fire at the offshore islands of Quemoy and Matsu displayed a fierce, if relatively harmless, posture. But both sides refrained from actions that might widen the conflict.

The line that divided Korea, however, did not hold until buttressed by a long and costly struggle. Korea revealed the responsibilities and costs of the American policy of collective security. At the Japanese surrender, the United States had allowed the Soviet Union to occupy the territory north of the thirty-eighth parallel until elections under United Nations supervision would decide the liberated country's future. The Russians promptly installed a repressive puppet regime that booted out the UN observers and made free elections impossible. Nevertheless, the Americans refrained from arming the southern government because the peninsula had no significant economic, military, or political value to the United

States. Indeed, Secretary of State Dean Acheson publicly stated that Korea lay outside the national defense perimeter.

The brutal invasion in clear violation of agreement compelled the United States to respond — not out of delusions about South Korean democracy, nor out of revulsion against North Korean dictatorship, but simply in the effort to salvage a shred of legality in a world verging toward uninhibited use of force. The accident of Russian abstention permitted action in the name of the United Nations, but the United States almost alone bore the costs in terms of money and manpower.

Harry Truman had to tread a narrow path to focus attention upon the purpose of the conflict. Outraged intellectuals such as Bertrand Russell had urged the immediate use of the atomic bomb against the Russians, once and for all to eliminate future threats to peace; and that quick way out of the dilemma may occasionally have tempted the president. Then too, he had to consider a long American military tradition according to which victory rewarded the army that applied maximum force to the total destruction of the enemy. General Douglas MacArthur, popular and ruthlessly competent, knew no other way to fight, particularly after the Chinese openly intervened to rescue the faltering North Korean regime. He sought permission to pursue his opponents, first across the thirty-eighth parallel and then into their sanctuaries beyond the Chinese boundary. Truman, insistent upon limiting the conflict, held back and finally demanded MacArthur's resignation. On the other hand, the president also had to resist pressure from a battle-weary public and from critics who wished an end to the bloodshed, even at the cost of enslaving thousands of Koreans. The combination of determination and restraint meant that the fighting would continue until the enemy withdrew but also that there would be no clear-cut victory.

In the end only President Eisenhower's threat to use atomic arms brought the North Koreans to terms. The one gain — but a consequential one — was the demonstration that the United States would resist aggression and would do so in measured terms. The struggle never became a war, only a police action; and it ground to a halt in an armistice, not a peace settlement.

The Korean experience validated the concept of the boundary line as a measure of aggression. There was nothing sacrosanct about the thirty-eighth parallel, any more than there was about the Oder-Neisse, the Curzon, or any other division of the map — except that each was an agreed-on limit and therefore a test of belligerence. Other issues remained subjects of dispute, but the powers could avoid disastrous collisions so long as they respected the lines that separated them. To protect them, the United States entered upon an array of defensive pacts supplementary to NATO, in southeast and central Asia, and in the Western Hemisphere.

The test of American intentions came in 1956 in two events close in time. The modest reforms by which the Communist regime of Hungary attempted to cope with its internal difficulties evoked the anger of the Russians, who brutally invaded the country, ousted one group of Party chieftains, installed another, and summarily brushed aside objections in the United Nations. At about the same time, Britain, France, and Israel, acting in concert, attacked Egypt in a move to protect their Near Eastern interests. The United States, while conceding the legitimacy of some complaints against Colonel Gamal Abdel Nasser, forced its allies to withdraw from a patently aggressive action. "There can be no peace without law," said President Eisenhower. "And there can be no law if we work to invoke one code of international conduct for those we oppose, and another for our friends." By contrast to its stand on Suez, the United States could do no more than protest ineffectually against the Russian attack in Hungary, equally aggressive and unjustified in international law. The concept of liberation thus died; the Soviet Union could do what it wished within the boundaries set in 1945. But elsewhere the commitment to nonaggression displayed by the United States, even when its interests and those of its closest allies were at stake, strengthened collective security.

Aggression, clearly defined by lines on a map, blurred when it took the form of subversion. In Eastern Europe, the Communist organizations that had survived the war often served as vehicles for implementing Soviet policy. Similar cadres threatened the stability of France, Italy, Greece, and Turkey; and American policymakers lacked guidelines on how to counter the threat. Massive economic assistance enabled some regimes to develop enough internal strength to contain the danger. Aid to Yugoslavia also forestalled any Soviet effort to bring Tito into line. Such steps were clearly within the accepted bounds of international law. So too was military assistance at the request of friendly governments, as when the United States intervened to restore stability in Greece and Turkey and helped establish order in Lebanon in 1958 and in the Dominican Republic in 1965.

In Iran and Guatemala, American counterinsurgency efforts staved off or ousted rulers susceptible to Communist control by means that were more ambiguous. Americans were not particularly skilled at practices out of accord with traditional diplomacy. Ill prepared for covert undertakings requiring secrecy and sophistication, the United States sometimes faltered, as it did in the Bay of Pigs fiasco, after which it stood by ineffectually while Fidel Castro betrayed the democratic revolution in Cuba.

Clumsy and costly as such measures were, they helped sustain the concept of an established line, the crossing of which affected not the immediate victims only but all nations. The speech President John F. Kennedy brought to Dallas in November 1963 clearly spelled out the special burden that the United States bore in defense of collective security. Moving "beyond the traditional roles of our military forces," he explained, the country had "achieved an increase of nearly 600 percent" in its special forces — "those forces that are prepared to work with our Allies and friends against the guerrillas, saboteurs, insurgents and assassins who threaten freedom in a less direct but equally dangerous manner. We in this country, in this generation, are, by destiny rather than choice, the watchmen on the walls of world freedom. We ask, therefore, that we may be worthy of our power and responsibility, that we may exercise our strength with wisdom and restraint, and that we may achieve in our time and for all time the ancient vision of 'peace on earth, good will toward men.' "

The policy those words expressed had already begun to come apart when the assassin's bullets prevented Kennedy from uttering them. Inconsistency and lack of support at home and abroad ate away at the resolve to sustain this costly, painful, and inconclusive approach to world problems. Collective security required the United States to remain on the defensive, ever on guard, ready to respond to aggressive acts anywhere, without taking the initiative and without overreaction that might spread hostilities. The policy required restraint and the willingness to pay the price — alone if necessary.

A subtle change in Communist policy substantially increased the burden. Down through the 1950s, the conventional Marxist understanding of history envisioned a steady deterioration of the capitalist economies, a steady strengthening of the Soviet productive system. At some point in the imminent future, internal contradictions would produce a crisis in the West and a proletarian revolution from within. At that point, no more would be necessary than fraternal assistance to prevent counterrevolution by reactionary elements. But the scenario had not unfolded as the Marxist writ dictated. Despite the loss of their empires and despite the damages of war, Britain, France, West Germany, and Italy had recovered and moved toward unprecedented prosperity, while the Russian economy, plagued by difficulties, lumbered from crisis to crisis. The collapse of capitalism would not soon come of itself, but would require nudges from without, and particularly in the exposed areas where the status quo was most vulnerable. Intermittent pressure substantially increased the burden of collective security.

Yet already, in the 1950s, those irked by the burden conjured up tantalizing visions of less expensive means of attaining the same ends — more bang for the buck, as Eisenhower's secretary of defense put it. Manpower superiority and geopolitical position permitted the Soviet Union to apply force in support of its friends anywhere along its frontier. The United States had to be ready everywhere. Rather than man every outpost at which an attack might come, it might well be less costly, and as effective, to restrain aggression by brandishing strategic weapons that could hit back at the enemy directly. By the 1960s the doctrine of mutual assured destruction (MAD) provided a potential, though frightening, alternative to collective security.

Although President Kennedy acquiesced, he understood the danger of nuclear confrontation that came perilously close to actuality during the Cuban missile crisis of 1962. The B-47s had then lined the runways, bays loaded with atomic bombs, capable of touching off a holocaust. To avoid a recurrence and yet be able to act, the United States needed the capability to fight brushfire wars, so that no future chief executive would have to choose between yielding to force and the horrors of atomic war.

As it happened, the brushfire war unfolded in Indochina, an area of small states left unstable by termination of the French protectorate. In Laos a revolutionary force challenged the internationally recognized regime in a conflict that shifted indecisively across an ill-defined border. But in Vietnam a clear line separated North from South, a line of the same validity as those in Korea and Germany. Americans initially perceived that the attacks from the North were identical in character with those the Communists had unsuccessfully launched elsewhere. Such is the eagerness to forget that it would be hard to find anyone today who will admit to having taken that stance in the 1960s. Nevertheless, at first there was practically no dissent from the American obligation to resist aggression in Vietnam, as elsewhere. Indeed, through 1964 the only debatable issue, as in the case of Korea, was whether to resist with restraint, applying only enough force to deter further aggression, or to carry the battle all out to the total destruction of the enemy. There is little doubt but that Congress, had it been asked, would have declared war, had not Presidents Kennedy and Johnson chosen the course of measured response, in the hope that a show of determination would induce the North Vietnamese to withdraw.

Unanimity dissolved in the latter part of the decade; and collective security as the core of American foreign policy crumbled with it. Public-opinion polls revealed that popular understanding and support for the war, though dwindling, endured through 1972. But well before then the government had lost the resolution and the capacity for sustaining the conflict.

The international consensus went first. The United Nations proved totally ineffective: the International Control Commission set up to keep the contending forces apart cynically evaded its responsibilities; the General Assembly refused to consider the issue; and the Russians forestalled action in the Security Council. In any case, the United Nations could have done little. The neutrals scrambled to avoid judgment. Some leaders, like Prime Minister Indira Ghandi of India, privately expressed sympathy but balked at taking a public stand. Others, like Prime Minister Olof Palme of Sweden, took refuge in convoluted praise of the heroic and socialist North Vietnamese peasants. For reasons of their own, the French turned their back on the conflict and even Britain decided to stand aside. Apart from aid by a few Asian allies, the United States bore the whole human and financial cost of the struggle.

Internal dissent erupted as those costs mounted. The news, freely and immediately reported, brought the battlefields into every home. The conflict dragged on, seemingly endless. Perhaps a compromise was possible, or a coalition government. President Johnson, poring over the choice of targets, worried about how to make bombing humanitarian. Only a few years from his death, he sank into despondency. Although majority opinion was still favorable, he could not cope with the problem of how to secure support from the opposition minority in a democracy. In effect he gave up; and the concept of collective security as the keystone of international law lay buried in the ruins of Vietnam. The very phrase "collective security" dropped out of political usage.

The Nixon administration substituted for it the classically conceived policy of balance of power. Shaking off the Vietnamese albatross and reducing American commitments in many parts of the world, it pursued détente, aiming to reduce conflict by long, involved negotiations to limit strategic and conventional arms, and by creating areas of common interest through trade to give the Soviets a stake in peace. The ineffectiveness of that policy in establishing adequate restraints on the Soviet Union generated a sense of helplessness in the 1970s. The West formally recognized the status quo in Eastern and Central Europe in return for the empty human-rights promises of Helsinki and did so while the Russians brutally stamped out dissent. Within the United States, spasmodic, ad hoc reactions to particular events revealed the absence of consensus on general policy.

The consequences appeared both at home and abroad. Attention turned inward upon the numerous genuine domestic problems, although the yearning for isolationism was out of accord with the realities of the interdependent world of the 1980s. Americans were not insensitive to the fact that famine and war ravaged much of Africa and Asia and some parts of the Western Hemisphere; but at least the distant victims could be shut out of mind.

Out there in the wider world, the concept of the binding quality of international law disappeared. Small states grew skeptical about the possibilities for peaceful redress of their grievances. Uninhibited by fear of sanctions, desperate, they moved boldly in behalf of their own interests — sometimes with justification, sometimes without. Israel thus intruded on Argentine territory in order to lay hands on the Nazi war criminal Adolf Eichmann. Iceland unilaterally extended its offshore boundaries to protect its economy despite the damage to British and German fisheries. But the justification often wore thin. Libya became a staging area for international terrorism. The behavior of Idi Amin led to an invasion of Uganda by the troops of his neighbors. Ayatollah Ruhollah Khomeini simply stated that no rules were binding in Iran other than those he himself derived from the Koran. Terrorism, the seizure of hostages, and the invasion of embassies became commonplace. Everywhere force ruled, inhibited only by the fear of counterforce. There was no longer even a pretense that the United Nations acted by any rules other than the individual interests of its members.

Moving through a world without standards or laws, Americans, like others, act like figures in a nightmare. Without guidelines, each nation seeks to save itself. Neutralism attracts some governments and their peoples, who hope that, as bystanders, they can escape the damage in a conflict of the big powers, which they cannot affect. Others find Finlandization attractive: they seek the patronage of a great neighbor in return for protection. Both courses are hazardous to all; and both make it impossible for anyone to take any action against aggression.

Thus the world drifts out of a dream and into a nightmare. Perhaps it never was realistic to expect, among sovereign states, adherence to a rule of law, even at the simplest level of respect for agreed-upon boundaries. But the actual ominous consequence of surrender of that expectation is a staggering increase in the potential for destruction everywhere

— and the widening margin of probability of disaster. Teetering now at the brink, it is worth recalling that for two decades, though at great cost, collective security kept much of the world free and at peace. The reasons for abandonment of that policy are worth pondering if we are to restore even that thin margin of safety.

2

One World

On April 8, 1943, Simon & Schuster published Wendell Willkie's little volume describing his trip around the world the previous year. In less than four months *One World* sold 1.55 million copies and soon thereafter appeared in translation in every major Western language. It was on its way to Hollywood when the death of its author aborted its transfiguration into a movie.

The popularity of the book derived neither from its literary quality nor from the acuteness of its perceptions, but rather from the clear, simple message it delivered. Its title stated the theme: the equality of men and nations. Willkie expressed the faith "that men and women like ourselves in other lands are fit to be free," and that, if helped to freedom, they would govern themselves wisely and well, a necessary precondition of the ability of all to unite in preserving peace through collective security.

The response of American readers reflected weariness with the war, eagerness to prevent a recurrence. Isolationist sentiment that only a few years before had directed national policy into channels of neutrality had ebbed away. Other books soon repeated Willkie's theme: Francis C. Capozzi called his homily *One World and One God* (1945); in the same year, the philosopher Ralph Barton Perry described *One World in the Making;* William George Carr used that identical title for his account of the United Nations (1946); and Dexter Masters and Katharine Way edited a collection, *One World or None* (1946).

Political sentiment also shifted. In 1944 Harold Stassen called for a world parliament. Assistant Secretary of State Sumner Welles urged the United Nations to draw up a postwar program "for policing the world against new aggression" and for international economic cooperation. A powerful current took form in the Congress to reverse the attitudes of neutrality of the 1930s. By a vote of 85 to 5, the Senate in the Connally Resolution urged the United States to join in establishing an international authority "with power to prevent aggression and maintain the peace of the world" — a far cry from the sentiment of 1919 that doomed Wilson's League of Nations.

The transformation was not as abrupt as at first sight it seemed to be. Though punctuated by periods of isolation, as in the 1920s and 1930s, the tradition of involvement in the welfare of peoples outside the United States extended back through the whole history of the Republic — indeed, in a significant sense, even antedated Independence. Intellectual and economic components always strengthened the conviction that Americans could not exist detached from affairs elsewhere, that they inhabited one globe of interdependent parts.

The earliest arrivals put an ocean between themselves and Europe; but they did not regard themselves as having abandoned the Old World. They planted their settlements in the wilderness not as a means of escape but — as John Winthrop put it — to build a city on a hill that would be a model men and women everywhere could emulate, as all approached the common destiny awaiting them at the second coming of Christ.

The commitments to involvement persisted long after seventeenth-century theological certainties faded away. The generation that conducted the American Revolution was no less convinced than the Puritans had been that its cause was the cause of all mankind; Jefferson and his contemporaries knew that progress was inevitable, that they led the way, and that others would follow — all others, everywhere around the earth. Hence they left the name of their country open-ended. The term *United States of America* did not confine their imaginations to the distance between New Hampshire and Georgia, but could extend indefinitely from Alaska to the Falklands and some day to the Eastern Hemisphere as well.

Thinkers in Jefferson's time did not presume to say whether ultimately one republic or several or many would govern all these territories, for although they believed in written constitutions, they also believed that each generation would compose its own frame of government. Firm believers in progress considered it ludicrous for the citizens of one era, even their own, to prescribe rules for those of later ones, who would certainly be more enlightened, more advanced, and wiser. But reason nevertheless informed the Founding Fathers that all humans moved in the same direction and therefore moved from the inherited diversities of the past to the developing unity of the future.

In the increasingly complex nation of the nineteenth century, the intellectual commitments to American involvement in the one world of which it was a part took various forms. The religious obligation to redeem the souls of distant strangers living in outer darkness moved Yankee women in hundreds of little farm villages to scrimp on their household expenditures and to contribute their mites to the cause. They thereby helped to establish a vast, voluntary array of missionary activities devoted not only to the salvation but also to the earthly health, education, vocational training, and welfare of remote areas of Africa, Asia, Latin America, and Europe. Dedication to those tasks animated Josiah Strong's immensely popular *Our Country* (1886), which explained that God had two hands: with one he prepared in the United States "the die with which to stamp the nations"; with the other he prepared mankind to receive its impress.

The secular version of this ideology was manifest destiny. The circumstance of settlement in a virgin land had nurtured a new kind of society and a new form of government dedicated to popular liberty. The American way would inevitably spread to neighboring areas and in diffusion grow increasingly attractive. Expansion would not depend on conquest; the manifest attractions of freedom would generate among Mexicans and Canadians and, in time, among all other peoples, the spontaneous desire to cast aside outmoded institutions, adopt the same forms, and join in common citizenship. The United States would intervene in the process only to prevent corrupt rulers from standing in the way. In 1874 Senator Charles Sumner of Massachusetts published a collection of *Prophetic Voices Concerning America* that drew together evidence of his country's continuing commitment to the diffusion of free institutions throughout the world. And that sense of involvement endured beyond the end of the century.

Ideologues from Winthrop to Strong, from Jefferson to Sumner could not depart from these attitudes. They valued ideas, and their fundamental beliefs as Christians and as heirs to the Enlightenment persuaded them that all humans descended from a common pair of ancestors and were therefore genetically identical. Genius could appear in any race, in any clime. The brotherhood of men, all men, followed from the fatherhood of God, one God. Whatever variants existed among humans had developed since the Creation some four thousand years earlier, were the products of differences in environment, and would recede in importance under the beneficent influence of free institutions.

To hold an idea, of course, was not the same as to act upon it; a gap between belief and practice remained. Distance enabled Americans to shake their fists at the despotism of the Hapsburgs and the Romanoffs, even to twist the tail of the British lion, without the obligation of following through with action. Indeed a time perspective that pushed expected results off to the distant future made it all the easier to adhere to the faith in universal unity. On the rare occasion that called for an immediate measure, caution verged on timidity.

That was the dilemma of Secretary of State Henry Clay in 1826. Himself an heir to Jefferson, he had been a leader of the expansionist war hawks in 1812, had devised the American system, and had sponsored the national road. He did not doubt his country's future spread. But he worried: When would the future arrive? The colonists in Spain's American possessions had indeed emulated the patriots of 1776, had proclaimed and won their independence, and were ready to form democratic governments. Now the Liberator, Simón Bolívar, called a meeting in Panama of all the New World's free states, and among them, of course, the mother of republics in the north. Long-held visions of ultimate union made Clay reluctant to reject the invitation; awareness of profound immediate cultural and social differences made him reluctant to accept it. He got the best of both courses. He accepted; but procrastination put off congressional approval so that the delegates reached Panama too late to participate, thus satisfying both vision and reality.

Clay's acumen prevented a more drastic rejection — as when, a century later, the United States turned aside from the League of Nations. But Americans did not, even in the isolationist 1920s and 1930s dissolve their nonpolitical links with the outer world; indeed, they then strengthened their economic ties, as well as their overseas missions and educational, medical, and vocational institutions. For years also, reformers, labor leaders, socialists, and humanitarians insisted that all existing states would someday merge. Although the internationalists were vague about the means of approaching it, the vision they perceived on the distant horizon was luminously clear and attractive.

Desertions from the faith in one world occurred toward the end of the nineteenth century among some intellectuals, who abandoned the belief in the unity of the human species. The spread of evolutionary ideas changed ways of thinking about the age of the earth; the past reached back millions of years, instead of a few thousand — so eradication of physical and cultural differences among peoples might not be a quick or simple matter. Indeed it might not be possible at all.

Domestic issues in the South, in California, and in the great cities strengthened the scientific and cultural force of racism. The suggestion that immutable genetic traits divided mankind into superior and inferior races justified inequality and temporarily satisfied Americans threatened by the blacks, the Chinese, and the new immigrants from southern and eastern Europe.

Racism had troublesome implications for American attitudes toward the outer world as well. Citizens who would not treat blacks or Japanese or Jews or Italians as fully equal in Alabama or California or New York or Chicago could not conceive of adding to the numbers of such people made fully equal by annexation. Yet from the start of the Republic, territorial expansion — whether by purchase in Louisiana and Alaska, by conquest in New Mexico, or by treaty in Hawaii — had made annexed areas integral parts of the United States and had entitled their residents to all the privileges and immunities of citizens. Racists could only contemplate further expansion if they could rule the inferior breeds as subjects rather than share power with them. The times therefore called for the acquisition not of territories but of colonies. In the 1890s influential imperialists who advocated that policy commanded widespread attention and distorted the relationship between the United States and the rest of the world.

The imperialists, between 1890 and 1914, vociferously urged a laggard nation to acquire colonial possessions. The other countries were doing it; and the United States had to follow if it was to attain a global position commensurate with its size, wealth, and potential power. The question in Hawaii, Samoa, even Tangier and Morocco was not simply whether the United States should intervene as opposed to allowing those areas to remain independent: if the United States did not intervene, such areas would come under the control of Germany or Japan or Britain. The record of the past, as imperialists read it, was littered with the wreckage of civilizations too flabby to defend themselves. Besides, it was a duty to spread the advantages of Americanism to the inferior peoples ready to be grateful. Besides too, it would be profitable — to commerce, to industry, to agriculture. It was time, therefore, to shed the republican distinctiveness and anti-colonial scruples inherited from the eighteenth century and to compete with others for the spaces on the map that would determine the world's future.

The imperialists gained in political strength until 1900. Strategically situated in the administration elected in 1896, they took advantage of the Spanish-American War to thrust the country into acquisitions in the Caribbean and in the Philippines. The election of 1900 kept in office the government responsible for those territorial gains. And shortly thereafter, the assassination of President McKinley advanced to the White House Theodore Roosevelt, a leading exponent of the strenuous life of imperialism. The way seemed then open to further gains.

Nevertheless, for all the Roughrider's thrashing about in Panama and the Caribbean, American overseas expansion ceased. Instead there began an uncomfortable, embarrassed process of withdrawal from the possessions seized in the splendid little war. On a map of the world in 1914 the United States was behind — not only behind the great powers, England, France, Germany, but also behind Japan, Italy, Belgium, Portugal, and the Netherlands. And in later years America blithely passed by the opportunities for territorial gain presented by the two world wars.

Imperialism, dramatic as an ideology, had little effect upon action. Its most influential exponents around the turn of the century — Brooks Adams, Alfred T. Mahan, Theodore Roosevelt, Henry Cabot Lodge, John Hay, and Albert J. Beveridge — were neither businessmen nor politicians of the usual sort. They were intellectuals, men of ideas, who considered power an instrument with which to give reality to words. They understood the need to find allies among large segments of the population, and therefore couched their arguments in terms they hoped would mobilize such support. But they did not represent those they addressed. They watched their country's withdrawal after 1900 with a dismay matched only by the impatience with which they had earlier observed its hesitation in joining the competition for empire. Their polemics mingled passionate appeals to the interest of businessmen, farmers, and Christians, with a furious contempt for those who remained deaf to the summons.

The imperialists did not understand that the rejection of colonies was not a withdrawal from the world. Americans did not wish to be the rulers of subject peoples, but did continue to support a vast array of overseas educational, philanthropic, and religious enterprises. And citizens of the United States expanded their economic activities in a fashion consistent not with imperialism but with the concept of one world within which men and women could move without government interference. In the quarter-century between 1890 and 1914, most people consistently judged political systems by the degree to which they facilitated relationships among individuals.

Overseas commerce, on which much of the American economy had long rested, was by its nature cosmopolitan. The very act of trade created interdependence; Bostonians or Philadelphians familiar with the coasts of the Mediterranean and the Baltic or at home in the Cape and Canton could not think in narrow terms. Early diplomacy after Independence embraced the theme of mercantile harmony. Americans knew that their republic differed from all other states, but believed they could conduct mutually advantageous trade with anyone. They would make no treaties of alliance; they remained eager to form commercial agreements.

Toward the end of the nineteenth century, attitudes expressed not in words but in acts revealed a deepened sense of connectedness. Americans looked toward a future organized neither by detached, totally sovereign states nor by some fanciful world government; rather, they envisioned one world that would give ample scope to the operations of individuals but would rarely depend upon the intervention of any political entity. Various portions of the globe would concentrate on the products for which nature had fitted them, while commerce bound them all together.

Clues to the nature of America's economic relations to the outer world showed up in the patterns of its foreign investments and trade. Imperialist motives did not determine the flow of capital. The direction actually taken revealed better than verbal pronouncements that the country faced outward, but not toward colonies.

In 1914 the direct foreign investment of the United States was still small compared to that of Britain, France, or Germany. It amounted in all to little more than $2.5 billion. But considered in the context of existing resources, that was a large sum: the equivalent of about 7 percent of the American gross national product. The percentage was about the same as it would be in 1960 or 1980 — a significant indication of the importance foreign investment had already attained. Any thought of isolation or of detachment from the world beyond the national frontiers was fanciful.

Investment for the most part did not follow along lines advocated by the imperialists, who sought colonies in strategically located, backward countries with abundant raw materials and cheap labor for exploitation. United States exports faced no competition in such places, and weak indigenous governments and docile natives facilitated conquest as well as good works and conversion to the proper faith. Africa, Asia, and the Caribbean region most closely matched the terms of this familiar description.

But these were the areas to which capital from the United States did not flow. In all of Africa, with which the United States had had some contact since the establishment of Liberia and, in a sense, since the seventeenth century, American investment amounted to only $13.5 million — a minuscule sum. In Asia (including for these computations everything from Turkey in the west to the Philippines and Australia in the east), the total amounted to some $120 million — a larger sum than for Africa, but still less than 5 percent of the whole. And this, fifteen years after the Battle of Manila Bay, five decades after Commodore Perry's opening of Japan, and after a century of close contact with China. Moreover, investments in both Africa and Asia were mercantile rather than exploitative, consisting of stock-in-trade and of distribution facilities. These commercial activities continued patterns that had existed in the same areas since Independence.

Even in the Caribbean, where the situation was slightly different, expansion did not take the form fancied by imperialists. There, the great adventure of 1898 had begun; there the United States held important possessions — Puerto Rico, the Virgin Islands, the Canal Zone — and there it also dominated nominally independent countries like Cuba, Haiti, and Nicaragua. In the whole region — and adding thereto all of South America — the total American investment amounted to about $700 million — substantial, though not overwhelming. In this area also, as in Asia and Africa, capital consisted primarily of commercial distribution facilities, with only secondary attention to the exploitation of natural resources. The four continents that imperialists defined as backward and fit for colonial development, taken together, thus absorbed only about a third of American foreign investments, and not in the form the imperialists considered appropriate.

Investments in the northern and southern neighbors of the United States were far more important. Canada and Mexico between them absorbed more than $1 billion in American capital; and paradoxically that occurred precisely when the old nineteenth-century manifest destiny visions of annexing both countries finally disappeared. While Americans regarded Canada and Mexico as extensions of the domestic market, the independence of those bordering nations was more secure than ever. Investment emphasized distribution, although the Canadian protective tariff persuaded some manufacturers to establish branches north of the border, and mining and ranching attracted some speculators to the south. Proximity and long, largely open frontiers counted for more than imperialist ideology.

More surprising was diversion of a sum almost as large to a region where involvement made no sense whatever from an ideological point of view. In 1914 Americans had investments of more than $600 million in Europe — about a quarter of their total overseas holdings. Whatever else the citizens of the New World believed of the Old, they hardly considered it backward, or susceptible to exploitation, or open to conquest as a colony. In sending their dollars eastward across the Atlantic, therefore, they rejected a basic imperialist premise that capital would flow from the more developed to the less developed places of the earth and that political power would expand with it. Furthermore, Americans thus invested in an area that itself exported capital elsewhere; they sent dollars to England while Britain dispatched pounds to Argentina and, indeed, to the United States. The trend, unmistakable, grew steadily and continued after 1914 to the 1970s.

Neither imperial interests nor precise computations of profitability motivated Americans to invest as they did. Far more important were beliefs about the relation of their country to the world — beliefs held in the first instance by the small minority who actually made investment decisions, but diffused with greater or lesser intensity to wider segments of the population. The sources of the capital directed toward Europe revealed those beliefs.

As in the past, agricultural exports generated investment opportunities for intermediaries. The volume and value of the commodities shipped eastward across the Atlantic had risen steadily in the nineteenth century. By 1875 they equaled in value the total of American imports from Europe; and their increase thereafter turned the balance of trade positive. Farmers through the years and into the 1970s were well aware that their prosperity depended on distant markets; and surpluses left by the sale of grains, fibers, and meats were available for investment.

But at the beginning of the twentieth century, those products shared cargo space with new kinds of exports. Sophisticated goods made in the United States became prominent in Old World showrooms, although European manufacturers were still technically more advanced. Long before Jean-Jacques Servan-Schreiber voiced the fear, Englishmen heard warnings of the Yankee challenge. A book published in London in 1901 noted that "the American industrial invasion" had given the outsiders control of almost every industry created in the previous fifteen years. The chief new features of metropolitan life were "the telephone, the portable camera, the phonograph, the electric street car, the automobile, the typewriter, passenger lifts in houses, and the multi-plication of machine tools." In almost every one of these, the American maker was supreme; in several of them, he was the monopolist.

At the time, and thereafter, managerial skill, industrial leadership, and advanced technology seemed to account for the success of the American invasion. Undoubtedly, advanced technology contributed to the popularity in Europe of the McCormick reapers and Singer sewing machines, just as it later did for the products of Xerox and IBM. But that popularity did not fully explain the strenuous American efforts to find buyers in the Old World. Their home market was far from satiated, and investments in sales ventures abroad were only marginally profitable — rarely more profitable than comparable investments within the United States, and sometimes even more subject to sizable losses. Nevertheless, overseas markets remained attractive, for entrepreneurs attached a nonmonetary value to foreign speculative ventures, as they did to the display of goods in world expositions. Having succeeded at home, they wished to show competitive effectiveness against the best of the Old World in a demonstration of ability for which the prizes were prestige and self-esteem as much as dollars.

The effort to sell abroad sucked Americans into permanent investment. The initial steps generally involved contracts with local distributors, agents, and jobbers, which ran into difficulty precisely because profit margins were narrow or nonexistent. The Americans then responded by setting up either their own marketing organizations or branch manufacturing plants.

Soon the number who took the same path increased, and with it the volume of exported capital. The Pullman Palace Car Company, the McCormick Harvesting Machine Company, and the meatpackers came early; Standard Oil, Eastman Kodak, American Radiator, Western Electric, National Cash Register, Singer, and General Electric followed. By 1900 twenty-eight very large American plants operated in the Old World, along with some smaller ones; and some of them promptly set out to gobble up local competitors. "Sell out," the representatives of the American Match Trust warned the English stockholders of the Bryant & May Company in 1901, or "we will whip you out of your boots."

Fifty more American establishments of substantial size appeared across the Atlantic between 1900 and 1910 in response to European protectionism; and a parallel development transferred American life-insurance techniques to the Old World until restrictive legislation narrowed opportunities.

The investment process was thus far different from that imagined by the imperialists and accepted by subsequent historians deluded by their rhetoric. Backward countries, blessed with impoverished populations, with low costs, and with feudal governments, did not attract American entrepreneurs. The flow of capital was incidental to the effort to sell goods and services. Investors therefore valued a stable social and political environment, a population advanced enough to acquire new consumption habits, and a market prosperous enough to pay for expensive products not previously regarded as essential.

The entrepreneurs who embarked upon these hazardous foreign ventures often had to justify their decisions — to partners, to stockholders, and to themselves; and the records of their elaborate calculations appeared in company reports and in the internal correspondence of their firms. In the last analysis, investors always described their goal in the same terms: profit. Their arguments were appropriate to the image hardheaded businessmen held of themselves. There was indeed a case for going abroad to protect patents that foreign pirates might otherwise infringe; there was also a case for safeguarding the value of a trade name by the dispersed manufacture and service of complex machines. So too, antitrust laws that prevented expansion within the United States sometimes made it necessary to go elsewhere.

Still, many a businessman protested his hardheadedness too much. With investment, as with sales, there was rarely such evidence of surfeit at home as to make overseas outlets imperative. That there were alternative domestic uses for capital was evident from the fact that the United States continued to attract the investments of Europeans in sizable amounts.

Edward H. Harriman was one such hardheaded businessman, who would indignantly have rejected the epithet "romantic." He argued that he was utterly practical in the vision of a transportation system to girdle the globe. His ships would connect his rails, which traversed the American continent, with those he proposed to lay across China and Russia. Add a few lines in western Europe and some Atlantic steamers and the job would be done. As simple as that. With the same fanaticism, Willard Straight advanced his harebrained schemes for developing China.

Hidden by the words were men pursuing unadmitted dreams. Some such investors, having attained a kingly dignity in their own country, sought the larger realm in which to become emperors. Others strove with the determination of provincials to prove themselves not only against local competitors but against everyone, in an ever-widening planetary metropolis. Nothing — not even national boundaries — would circumscribe their endeavors.

Out of these experiences developed a new kind of corporation that did business in a fashion independent of political lines. No theory described it in advance. Its traits emerged from specific circumstances — discontinuous, abrupt, and without any effort to pursue the implications. For instance, the Western Electric agent in Bangkok reported in 1907 that the anti-American attitude of the government of Siam stood in the way of an order. The corporation's vice-president responded that Western Electric had factories in Great Britain, Belgium, Germany, France, Russia, Austria, Italy, and Japan — so it was international rather than American and "could arrange to have the order go to any one of those countries that might be preferred." This ad hoc response to a specific problem contained the seed of a concept that flowered after 1918 — one that regarded private enterprise abroad as somehow, somewhat, detached from the government of the area in which it operated. Ford could as well produce in the Soviet Union as in Britain or Germany.

The new conditions called for new ways of doing business. Handbooks, manuals, and directories of international trade showed the importance of detailed, precise, current information in increasingly sophisticated form from every corner of the earth. The desirability of academic training to handle this knowledge evoked calls for systematic instruction in international trade in schools and universities. And the desire for cooperation to enlighten entrepreneurs about overseas opportunities culminated in the formation in 1914 of the National Foreign Trade Convention.

Americans involved in international transactions consistently pressed global considerations upon their government. The inadequacies of the banking system gave them continuing concern. Until the Federal Reserve Act, national banks could establish no branches, effect no foreign transactions, because anachronistic laws permitted them to do business only over the counter at the places named in their charters. Only after the creation of an international monetary and banking system at the Bretton Woods Conference (1944) did the old barriers drop away.

Cautiously the United States entered into agreements with other states to facilitate business. Heroic efforts aimed to establish the uniformity of consular invoices — the ideal, a slip of paper that would bear an identical meaning in every part of the world. Some hopes of improving global communications focused on the International Chamber of Commerce that held its first session in Liège in 1905. Seven years before they felt the need to form their own United States Chamber of Commerce, Americans participated enthusiastically in the international body. The world organization's fifth congress, held in Boston in 1912, stressed the mutuality of commercial interests that transcended national lines. Charles Nagel, the United States' secretary of commerce and labor, pointed out that "improved methods of communication" brought everyone together and helped all realize that there was "no such thing as ultimate advantage at the expense" of a neighbor. Rules of the game to govern all transactions equitably were, in his judgment, "even more important than agreements arrived at as a result of diplomatic negotiations." The businessmen of the world had to establish "a relation so intimate commercially, and ultimately socially" that no country could afford controversy.

As a matter of course, therefore, business people were for peace. Prominent but atypical figures — Edward A. Filene, Andrew Carnegie, and Henry Ford among them — lent their names from time to time to the organized peace movement. More important, run-of-the-mill entrepreneurs, not likely to have radical associations, simply judged war bad for business, were impatient with ideological expressions of the martial spirit, and believed that their own prosperity depended on stable relations among all states.

Men who were not usually articulate, not theoretically minded, and only tangentially interested in the great issues of the period nevertheless revealed in their reactions to concrete questions a general view of their position in the world. They had arrived at a concept of one free world that stressed the primacy of economic interconnections above political forms and cultural norms. Their world was free in the sense that it encouraged the uninhibited decisions of investors, buyers, sellers, employers, and employees. That concept suffered from ambiguities and contradictory qualifications; but it evoked support from farmers, for whom it meant the freedom to ship their products to ever-expanding markets; from laborers, for whom it meant the freedom to migrate to where jobs were; and from thousands of petty entrepreneurs, who drew parallels with the freedom they sought in their own enterprises.

Thus understood, the idea of one world also offered Americans a means of restating and preserving the patriotic connotations of earlier beliefs — in the freedom of the seas, in the mercantile virtues, and in the manifest mission of a pilgrim people building a city upon the hill to redeem the world. The concept left a durable imprint upon the policy of the United States. It survived the impulse to isolation of the 1920s and 1930s, and after 1941 it meshed with the messianic idealism endemic to American rhetoric.

The notion thus supplied Wendell Willkie with the basic foundation for his belief in equality of peoples and states in *One World*. It also accounted for the conviction after 1945 that economic aid would lead other nations toward democracy and supply them with the means of participating in a universal enterprise. In 1947 invitations to participate in the

Marshall Plan went forth in good faith to the Soviet Union and its European satellites. Hardheaded businessmen sincerely thought that they could make deals with anyone to the mutual advantage of all. You can do business with the Russians! That was the message of Joseph E. Davies, once United States ambassador to the Soviet Union and (like Willkie) a corporation lawyer, whose book *Mission to Moscow* did become a popular Hollywood movie.

Hardheaded businessmen did not, however, reckon with the force of an alternative view of the world, held by people whose calculations took quite another form.

3

The Failure of Communism — and What It Meant

ON JULY 30, 1961, *Pravda* and *Izvestia* published the new draft program of the Communist party of the Soviet Union. Soon thereafter, readers of the Soviet newspapers learned that the document had been greeted with enormous enthusiasm. It answered "very important questions," in the sober opinion of a loyal Hungarian. It "assures our happiness," explained a molding-machine operator in Irkutsk. *Pravda* called it proof that "socialism has triumphed," and Premier Nikita Khrushchev read it in full at the Party congress in October.

The draft program ostensibly forecast the planned achievements of the next twenty years. The Russian people received the glad news that the next two decades would bring them unparalleled economic prosperity. At the end of that period, they learned, per capita real income would be up 250 percent, they would enjoy an abundance of housing, and free lunches, free rent, and free transportation — to each according to his needs.

Loyal Party members, along with sympathizers outside the Soviet Union, took this pronouncement at face value. The satellite countries, of course, hailed it as a veritable scientific forecast of what was to come; the neutrals gave it respectful and admiring attentions; and even Western journals, while confident that the free world would do as well, accepted the program for what it purported to be.

By 1980 the time was almost up. Yet there was no prospect that the Soviet Union would deliver on the promises of the draft program. The failure should not have surprised critical readers even in 1961. What was surprising was the fact that few found it necessary to wonder why the Party issued the new program when it did.

The answer to that question is critical to understanding the forces that shaped Soviet policy after 1961.

The closest parallel occurred just twenty-five years earlier. On June 22, 1936, the plenum of the Central Committee of the Communist party approved a new constitution for the Union of Soviet Socialist Republics. Six months later, after a pretense of discussion, the All-Union Congress of Soviets promulgated what Stalin described as "the only thoroughly democratic Constitution in the world." This charter of unprecedented liberality provided for free elections by universal suffrage in every organ of government, from the collective farm and the factory to the highest levels of state power. It gave the people unconditional guarantees of personal rights, including those to a public trial and defense by counsel. It established an independent judiciary and assured the citizens freedom of speech, press, assembly, and the privacy of correspondence.

The passage of time made it clear that the Soviet constitution of 1936 had a twofold aim. It aimed to gain foreign support in the period of the United Front. And it threw up a smoke screen that concealed the famine and the breakdown in agriculture that brought millions of Ukrainians to starvation; the purges and deportations that introduced the long Stalinist reign of terror; and the shift in foreign policy that culminated in the Nazi-Soviet pact of 1939. The utopian vision was a deliberate means of concealing developments that moved in precisely the opposite direction from that promised.

No one in 1961 could write with confidence of what then transpired behind the iron curtain. But significant bits of evidence indicated that the Soviet fantasies of future abundance served a function similar to that of the 1936 constitution. And the events of the two decades since publication of the draft program now amply confirm the suspicion that the roseate glow on that distant horizon was a means of distracting attention from the immediate failure of Communism. The Party leaders in 1961 confronted the collapse of earlier hopes and realigned state policy, with serious consequences for the rest of the world.

The most pronounced failure had occurred in the chosen field of Communist tactics — economic development — and particularly in that sector of it that bore most directly on the welfare of the people.

Such a conclusion at first sight ran counter to all that had been written about the strength of the Soviet productive system. The figures most readily available, for national income and for the output of certain industries, made a creditable showing indeed. Russian national income, for instance, rose from 54 billion rubles in 1950 to 144 billion in 1960 — a rate of growth greater than that of any Western European country. Measurements of the production of steel, cement, and other goods seemed equally favorable.

But we learned from Hitler to be skeptical of the quality of totalitarian economic miracles. The statistics themselves were suspect. In dictatorial societies, all information was contrived for a purpose that was as often concealment as enlightenment. The distortion or suppression of data arose partly from the wish to deceive outsiders, but also from the worries of inefficient bureaucrats fearful of their superiors, from the rivalry of competing agencies, and from the errors in a system that operated in secret and lacked any open checks.

In any case, the available statistics measured some but not all aspects of the productive system. The rise in national income showed that greater quantities of goods and services were being turned out, but did not in itself reveal whether the result made greater quantities available to consumers. A rise in steel or cement production could lead to an increase in the number of prisons or missile bases or homes. In the abstract calculation of output, the destination of the yield made no difference; but to the population of the country, the abstract calculation was less important than whether the result sheltered or enslaved them.

Yet it was precisely in relation to consumption patterns that information from the Soviet Union was most deficient. Analysts who attempted to go beyond the question of volume of production to that of what was produced and for whom found only scattered fragments of fact. Such fragments in 1961, however, pointed umistakably to the conclusion that the Communist system had not increased the supply of goods available to the people who lived under it. In 1980 the situation had scarcely improved; for the second successive year, a shortfall compelled the government to depend on grain imports. The frequency with which Soviet agriculture failed to sustain its population disclosed the fragility of the system.

In the summer of 1961 aggressive Communist pressures applied to East Germany glaringly exposed the deficiencies of the Soviet order. The Germans of the East zone had not then recovered from the damage of the war. Bled by their

Russian conquerors, their economy limped along until the outbreak of 1953. The repression that followed made the problem worse. By 1958 a crisis had set in. Published statistics that credited East Germany with a higher rate of economic growth than West Germany were poor comfort to people who could see on which side of the border the grass was greener; the numbers were more manageable than the actuality of the system that could not make a go of it. A substantial subsidy in toll charges from the Bonn regime did not help. Compelled to cut back on heavy industry such as aircraft and automobile production, the East German government still could not provide the necessities of life for the people. Shortages and calamitous disorders followed; and a steady stream of some 2.5 million refugees, attracted by the contrast in the West, deprived the country of its lifeblood. A tough response, with Russian support, staunched the flow in 1961: the wall, built in contravention of the four-power agreements regulating the status of Berlin, imprisoned the East Germans. Thereafter Western helplessness permitted the Communist masters to manage their population with the efficacy of a labor camp. In the 1970s subventions from the Federal Republic of Germany and from other Western nations provided the margin for some improvement in East Germany, as in the other East European satellites. Life nevertheless remained grim, although dubious statistics made all measurements suspect.

In 1980, and even more so in 1961, outsiders knew even less about the People's Republic of China. Despite the normalization of relations after 1972, that vast area remained hermetically sealed off from the rest of the world. Whatever fluctuations occurred in Chinese leadership and in Party line, news remained subject to tight control and travelers saw what the government intended them to see. The chief effect of the easier restrictions after Mao's time was revelation of the falsity of the accounts of smiles on peasant faces earlier reported by Jan Myrdal and other happy Western tourists.

Yet already in 1961 enough tragic details had trickled out to reveal the pattern of failure. And the rulers of 1980 only confirmed what the critics of 1961 had suggested. With ruthless determination, China's masters labored to industrialize the country, and they proudly pointed to impressive increases in some branches of production. But the overall effort was a costly failure. Despite earlier boasting, Peking in 1961 was silent on its output goals. The communes evoked tremendous resistance and fell far short of their objectives; and the attempt to transform the economy plunged agriculture into a prolonged crisis. Official revelations after the downfall of the Gang of Four confirmed earlier Western judgments that had been only the products of informed guesswork.

Famine, never a stranger to the country, acquired an endemic quality. In 1959, one-third, and in 1960, almost one-half of the arable land suffered from floods, hailstorms, and contamination. And in the summer of 1961, when a searing drought gripped Hupeh province, food ran short everywhere. That year and frequently thereafter necessity compelled the government to use scarce foreign exchange to purchase wheat from Canada and Australia. From time to time, higher education came to a halt, and orders from above sent students to rural areas to work in the fields. The cholera epidemic in Kwangtung province in August 1961 also reflected deteriorating living standards. There is no way of knowing whether two thousand or two million or twenty million Chinese starved in the three decades following World War II, but rations of food and clothing sometimes sank to the meanest levels of subsistence, according to retrospective accounts.

Most important, China was slow to confront the fundamental problem of population increase. Trapped by a dogmatic hostility to birth control and by a fanatic disregard of personal values, the Communist leaders long put off efforts to halt the rise in numbers. But the inability of the economy to grow rapidly enough to take care of ten million births a year (let alone to improve existing standards of living) slowly compelled the government to reconsider its approach — although with what effect remained unclear.

All the Soviet satellites, from Czechoslovakia, Bulgaria, and Hungary to North Vietnam, met similar problems. Most impressive of all, the Soviet Union itself — whatever show of strength it made to the outer world — still suffered from deficiencies, seriously aggravated by the great failures of the 1950s and 1960s. Despite Khrushchev's personal interest, or perhaps because of it, agricultural productivity did not increase enough to supply the demands of the population. The premier himself spoke frequently in the provinces in 1961 of his dissatisfaction with the output of foodstuffs, as well as of housing and other consumer goods. He had cause for concern. In 1953 there were fewer livestock than in 1928, and grain production was grossly inadequate. Progress in the next quarter-century was not enough to close the gap.

In 1954, after many years of effort, the inability to raise productivity persuaded the Soviet Union to increase the amount of land under cultivation. Hundreds of thousands of workers and machines drawn from elsewhere converted immense tracts of marginal soil in Siberia and southeastern Russia to agriculture. The results were disappointing. After

1958 the Virgin Lands, swept by dust storms and parched by lack of rain, made little return upon the capital and effort invested in them. In July 1970 Leonid Brezhnev, by then Party chairman, closed the accounts on more than a decade of unsuccessful effort, echoing, as he did so, his predecessor's complaints about past errors.

The nineteenth-century expansion of the American frontier met similar setbacks in the settlement of the Great Plains. But in the United States flexibility cushioned the economic system as a whole against the consequences of such mistakes. By contrast, the rigid planning of the Soviet Union transmitted the shock of failure to every sector of the productive system. When grain harvests fell short of their goals, the Russian people paid the cost.

The Soviet regime never confronted, much less solved, the housing problem. From the revolution it inherited an inadequate plant. Moscow and Leningrad were as poorly prepared to shelter an industrial proletariat as were other European cities. But the situation became worse rather than better in the interwar years. The number of urban residents grew rapidly while the share of national resources allocated to housing remained far smaller than in Western societies. The shortage of space was already acute when the German invasion added its destructive toll.

After the peace, the absolute necessity of repairing the war damage raised the share of capital invested in housing. But the result did not compensate either for older deficiencies or for new needs. The population of the Soviet Union continued to rise, from 196 million in 1940 to 212 million in 1960; and in the same period the proportion located in cities skyrocketed from 31 percent to 58 percent, with the steady shift of peasants to urban jobs. Yet only in 1957 and 1958 was there a substantial increase in construction rates, and that did not ease the shortage. In 1957 the total living space per person in urban areas was smaller than it had been in 1926. In the 1960s and 1970s the need to increase the housing stock received only intermittent attention; and Soviet citizens continued to suffer. The Russian proletarian, an honored figure in Communist mythology, was less well sheltered than his counterpart anywhere in the West.

Workers and peasants were just as poorly off with regard to the clothes they wore and their chance of owning an electric appliance. The planners paid but the scantiest attention to such desires, and the creaky distribution system raised the cost beyond reach. Only very meager crumbs of the increase in productivity reached the Russian people.

The inability to improve living standards may reflect some distortion in the published statistics. More likely, it was the result of Communist decisions about how to divide the economic pie and of miscalculations about the effects.

Any nation, by planning or free enterprise, can use its resources and labor to turn out goods its population will consume, or to sustain its military forces, or to create by capital investment the means of further production. It thus diverts energies directed at one goal from the others.

In 1928 the Soviet leaders, following the pattern set by the Czars, determined to hold military expenditures constant as far as possible, and to push heavy industry at the expense of consumer goods. They reckoned that an increase in power and productive capacity would reward the temporary sufferings of the Five-Year Plan. But the first plan led to a second and a third; when the war intervened, the day of the consumer had not yet come. Nor did peace alter the direction of development. In 1946 Stalin proclaimed a fifteen-year program of intensive industrialization along the same lines.

This policy was partly the product of history. From 1890 onward, the prominent economic role of the state, the pressure of military requirements, and the relatively large scale of enterprise had consistently favored investment in heavy industry in Russia, as against expansion of consumer markets. But the Bolsheviks in power had additional reason for furthering the tendency. Aware of the comparative backwardness of their economy, they determined to catch up with and outdistance the capitalist West, no matter what the cost to the Russian people. For they never doubted that the two systems would ultimately clash, and in their view, the final outcome rested primarily upon the relative strength of the rival economic orders.

The end of World War II imbued the Communist leaders with a sense of urgency. The contest for world domination seemed to approach a climax. The devastation of the six preceding years seemed to be the necessary catastrophe that, by Marxist thinking, would lead to redemption by revolution. The country, therefore, remained on a war footing, closed off from outside contacts and taught to fear the capitalist scapegoats who blocked the way to utopia.

The superior power of the West frustrated Stalin's dream of mastery. The defensive measures of the five years after 1947 contained the Communist threat in Greece, in Western Europe, and in Korea. Soviet tactics then shifted. Weariness after years of deprivation, the death of Stalin and the subsequent reduction of terror, the rise to prominence of new men like Georgi Malenkov, and the awareness that the collapse of capitalism was not imminent led to some modification of economic policy. The ultimate objective — the victory of Communism — never faded, but the means of attaining it changed.

The slogan of the new regime was "peaceful coexistence." The capitalist and Communist nations could live side by side without military encounter as long as the Soviet Union was strong enough to resist aggression. But the war between them would continue in another form: it would be a race for economic supremacy. In the first instance, the uncommitted nations would be the targets. The magnitude of the Soviet Union's achievements and the aid it would endeavor to give nonaligned states after 1954 would win them over by a display of the virtues of the Communist system. And in time the people of the capitalist countries would also perceive Soviet superiority and would gravitate spontaneously toward Communism. Their masters would be helpless to restrain them. Then would come the total world order of which the heirs of Marx dreamed.

This pattern of expectations left room for some improvement in living conditions. The general atmosphere of the thaw encouraged the hope that the Russian people might soon reap the rewards of earlier sacrifices. Above all, the vision of the Soviet Union as the showpiece of Communism demanded that outsiders receive a favorable impression of its life-style. The Five-Year Plan for 1955 to 1960 therefore showed more concern than preceding ones for housing and consumer goods — without, however, neglecting heavy industry. A great rise in productivity would cover needs of both kinds.

So ran the logic behind the Party's tactics in the years from 1953 to 1958. The Kremlin's adherence to this line depended upon three conditions. The arms stalemate between East and West permitted the diversion of a larger share of the national product to consumption without diminishing that which went into capital investment — hence the Soviet interest, in those years, in disarmament. The existence of a large and growing group of neutral nations unsympathetic toward capitalism nurtured the belief that Communism could spread without an open clash of arms. Most important, the Soviets, in peaceful competition, were to prove the superiority of their economic organization.

Lenin had, after all, long since demonstrated that the illusion of capitalist prosperity was only a product of imperialism. The living standard of the oppressed toilers in England, France, and the United States had not declined (as Marx had explained that it would) only because exploitation of colonial empires enabled their masters temporarily to indulge them in comparative well-being. With the prop of imperialism removed, the workers would soon become aware of the hardship of their lot. New data published by Soviet economists after the war confirmed the reliability of these predictions of what was to come. Meanwhile, the USSR, China, and the satellites would show that Communism could produce both a rising level of consumption and a high rate of economic growth.

After 1958 the dismal economic experience of the Communist regimes tempered these optimistic expectations. Moreover, the United States, Western Europe, and Japan enjoyed unparalleled abundance, despite their loss of colonies. The prospect that workers in New York or London or Tokyo would some day envy the lot of those in Moscow or Shanghai grew dim indeed.

Nor did the ruling circles in Egypt and India show any disposition to embrace Communism. They remained anti-American and anticapitalist, but they still fought the Communist party at home. Nasser did not hesitate to embrace his genial hosts in Moscow and at the same time jail their comrades in Cairo. Evidently it would take the use of the stick as well as of the carrot to tame the nonaligned nationalists in the future. In September 1961 the Russian press severely criticized Egyptian lack of appreciation for help in building the Aswan Dam.

In any case, it was a strain for the USSR to meet its mounting aid commitments, which in 1960 came to more than $1 billion. In the Sudan, Tunisia, Somalia, and Afghanistan, it was still necessary to bid against the West. Tension between the two greatest Communist powers led the Soviets to promise aid to North Korea, just as the Chinese did to Albania. But there was a marked cutback from the lavish promises of earlier, more confident years. In June 1961 the Kremlin refused to build the Euphrates Dam for the United Arab Republic and allowed the West Germans to step in. Red China, which had no other friends, fell from the roster of aid recipients in 1961. Significantly, Peking turned not to Russia, but to capitalist Australia and Canada for food.

Moreover, all did not go well with the projects on which the Soviets had already embarked. From many of the twenty-four countries that had signed economic agreements with the Soviet Union there were complaints — about badly designed petroleum equipment supplied to Argentina, about a hotel built in Rangoon but appropriate to the climate of Moscow, about a sugar plant in Indonesia, fine for Ukrainian beets but not for Javanese cane. In a flush of enthusiasm in 1958, the Soviet Union promised the Iraqi revolutionaries twenty-six industrial projects and a railroad. After a year, not one had been started, and the Iraqis murmured over the low quality and high prices of the goods received under their trade agreement.

Even when ventures turned out successfully, as did the Bhilai steel mill in India, the costs — and particularly the hidden charges — were high. The jovial Khrushchev was thought to have been joking, at a party for President Sukarno of Indonesia, when he showed his empty pockets and cried out, "Look, he took everything I had!" It may not have been funny at all.

Foreign aid was big business, and the Communists could not keep up with their rivals. The total promised by the Red bloc in the six years after 1954 came to about $5 billion, of which only about $200 million a year was actually delivered. By contrast, the United States alone actually paid out more than $56 billion between 1947 and 1961, and its allies in England, France, Germany, and Japan were moving into the field with increasing strength.

It was foolhardy for the Soviet Union to think it could do as well, particularly since the internal failures had placed excessive burdens on the economy. The gratification of some consumer desires after 1953 had cost too much and had called for complex organizational changes, by no means successfully carried through. What was worse, even a fleeting taste of the good things in life had raised the level of expectations. Youth, in particular, was restless. People no sooner got a flat in which to live than they wanted a television set and refrigerator to put into it and an automobile in which to escape from it. Glimpses of the style of life of the West through expositions and contact with foreigners stimulated these desires and threatened to dilute the cultivated image of the new Soviet man — selfless, devoted to work, and ready to sacrifice all for the Party goals.

The demands for foreign aid, consumption, and investment could not be met all at once. The forecasters, whose eyes were already on the 1960s, realized also that it would be difficult to sustain the high rate of growth of earlier decades. The low birthrate of the war years would be reflected twenty years later in a contraction of the productive age groups. With surface resources depleted, high-grade minerals would be more difficult to mine, obsolescence would become a serious problem, and a neglected transport system might not stand up to increased demands. And to maintain the same rate of growth called for an even higher rate of investment than earlier. The prospect that Communism would successfully meet all these challenges was far from bright.

Under these conditions, the Party congress of January 1959 scrapped the plan for 1955 to 1960 and adopted a new production program for the next seven years. The effort to raise living standards while still expanding heavy industry and supporting ambitious military and foreign aid programs had failed. The forecast for 1959 to 1965 was therefore much less ambitious. The new plan demanded a more thorough integration of the economies of the "socialist bloc" and it offered a preview of what awaited the Russian people in the 1960s. Priority went to heavy industry and chemicals; housing and consumer needs sank to the bottom in the order of urgency. Building, light industry, and food processing received the lowest rates of growth and the planners expected the volume of retail trade to decline — sure signs of an anticipated fall in real per capita incomes. Even the hope that increased leisure might compensate the people for commodities they would not receive proved illusory. The Economics Institute of the USSR Academy of Sciences learned in 1960 that hands drawn from domestic work and agriculture, joined with cadres of students, would have to strengthen the industrial labor force in order to meet production goals. The Russian people were again to pay the price for the growth of heavy industry.

The Kremlin could ascribe temporary failures to natural disasters. But the contrast with the free world's experience was nevertheless oppressive. The United States and England, France and Italy, West Germany and Japan steadily raised the standards of living of their populations. Convinced as they were of the infallibility of their doctrine, the Red leaders had to account for their inability to do as well.

The demand for an accounting was not then vocal, but was nonetheless real. In the Communist countries, the masses were politically helpless. The Chinese and East German regimes stifled every sign of opposition; and although the Soviet Union did not revert to the terror of the Stalinist years, censorship and control of opinion were thoroughly effective and dissent met swift reprisal. Yet men and women without adequate food, clothing, and housing were not efficient producers. Those who lived on nine hundred calories a day, as in China, simply could not summon up the energy to meet production quotas. And with the death of hope, apathy set in. Apart from the danger that the workers might resort to sabotage and might slack at work, blatant propaganda alone could not indefinitely sustain the efforts necessary for effective labor.

The loss of hope and of realizable objectives generated a quiet discontent most extreme at the points of contact with the superior achievements of the West. The very existence of West Berlin and Hong Kong, long irritating thorns in the sides of the Communist rulers, was graphic proof of the failure of Communism; hence, the ruthless closing of access to those places.

More important than popular discontent were grievances

within the Party cadres that contained the hard core of believers, among them all the important officeholders. The elaboration of governmental and Party services had created an army of clerks and officials, including by 1960 about 25 million white-collar employees in the Soviet Union. Their positions required specialized training and imposed upon some of them power and responsibility. Such men and women desired rewards commensurate with the risks they took and with their skills. After years of hardship and struggle they expected that their efforts would bring them whatever pleasures their society could afford. In 1948 Hungarian politburo members received luxury autos, villas, and unlimited checkbooks. They had no personal accounts but could draw any sum they wished from the national bank. The political leaders were aware of their dependence upon these elements of the population and realized that the means of coercion that kept men at the assembly line or peasants at their plows would not keep an engineer effectively at his drafting board or induce a manager to remain honest or to keep a plant producing efficiently. Deprived of incentives, the "workers of the brain" in their First Circles would become uncomfortably restive.

The elite, the new managerial classes, could not believe in the failure of their doctrine. Were the suspicion to spread that shortcomings were the fault of the leaders, it would weaken the very structure of authority. To forestall any such tendencies, the summer of 1961 witnessed a purge of the Central Committee of the Russian Communist party. Khrushchev soon shuffled off to retirement; and periodically, mysterious alterations of position changed the compositions of the Chinese, Polish, and Hungarian politburos.

Above all, the leaders themselves had to retain faith. As much as the necessity of quieting the populace and the

Party, their own psychological needs required them to explain their inability to reward their people as the capitalists had. Their way of thinking permitted them to see only two explanations. Marxist economics assured them that heavy industry was the foundation upon which all branches of production rested. If there were not enough shoes or homes, then greater investments in chemicals and steel were needed, even though such allocations, for the time being, increased the pinch on the consumer. And the hostile foreigner was long the scapegoat of Russian ills. Encirclement of the fatherland by capitalists bent on its destruction forced it to protect its people at the expense of their present well-being. Both explanations had the incidental virtue of justifying the increasing rigor of controls.

The Russians more readily embraced these myths because, for the first time, they gained on the West in overall military power. Communism was successful only in the ability to develop powerful machinery for war and for the related achievements in space. In July 1961, at the same time that the new draft program was devised, the Soviet arms budget rose by one-third.

The Communist leaders had drawn the appropriate conclusion. They had shifted tactics back to a power base. The phrases of peaceful coexistence lingered in their vocabulary, when useful. But what they no longer hoped to achieve by economic rivalry, they would attempt to achieve by force or the threat of force. No more now than earlier did they wish the holocaust of overt conflict; they continued to discuss disarmament while they built up their stock of weapons and resolutely opposed any suggestion of inspection. Meanwhile they vigorously attempted to win over the uncommitted governments in Asia, Africa, and South America and sought to neutralize the West by persuasive brandishment of bombs and rockets. Hence occurred the increasing expenditures for arms and the diversion of greater shares of the national product to capital investment. As for the people, they would wait for the draft program's pie in the sky — twenty years away.

By 1980 the twenty years had almost elapsed since announcement of the plan in 1961. The then-foreseeable had become past reality. Bedazzled visitors still brought back glowing accounts of what their own eyes had seen, while the unwelcome evidence of desperate refugees passed unheeded. Repression continued to hold dissent in check; the new class continued to further its interests; arms absorbed a growing percentage of the still creaky economy; negotiation remained a means of pursuing Soviet advantage while stalling the West; and neutralism continued to divide potential resistance while exposing the weakest peoples to Soviet aggression, directly or through surrogates.

4

The Gullibility of the Neutrals

THAT HARDHEADED BUSINESSMAN Andrew Carnegie put up the money to build the peace palace at The Hague; but in 1910, when it came to establishing the Endowment for International Peace, he had a question about the future: What would happen to the Endowment's capital when war became unthinkable, as it shortly would?

The faith on which that question rested made sense in the context of the one world approaching. War simply did not pay — anyone. Mutual accommodation for mutual advantage would soon replace that ancient barbarism. Men and nations collectively would condemn violence, and a code of international law would define proper behavior.

Carnegie could not imagine that two world wars would shortly find such confidence sadly wanting. But the Americans who lived through those exhausting conflicts hoped afterwards to prevent a repetition through collective security, so that future aggressors would face not one victim in isolation but the united force of all civilized nations, who were aware that a breach of the peace threatened the security of all. The evolution of a code of international conduct, backed by such sanctions, would make the bloody conflicts of the past impossible.

Countries that stood aside, that refused to make judgments as between aggressors and victims, undermined both collective security and law, and shortsightedly chose immediate as against general interests. Whether they gained or lost individually, they hampered the effort to preserve peace. Yet once the recollection of World War II faded, neutralism exercised a fatal attraction for many.

It is October 1962. The old man on the television screen blinks in bewilderment. Fatigue shows in the droop of his eyelids, in his hesitant choice of words as he expresses dismay. Jawaharlal Nehru, prime minister of India, speculates on the meaning of the Red Chinese invasion of his country. Abruptly, the camera shifts to banner-carrying demonstrators marching through a city street, to scrawny volunteers at a recruiting station, to women offering their jewels to the nation. Then come some old clips of the Dalai Lama, Tibet, mountains. For almost a decade, Nehru had refused to believe it could happen. In 1954 he had agreed with Chou En-lai's five principles of *panch sila* ("peaceful coexistence"), then had stubbornly clung to faith in peaceful Communist intentions despite the evidence in Korea and Indochina. In the very year of the agreement, the Chinese had begun to build a road across territory the Indians claimed. But Nehru made no issue of it. The seizure of Tibet, the crossing of the McMahon Line, and numerous minor provocations he explained away as misunderstandings among friends. But he could not explain away the newest act of aggression; thousands of ill-prepared Indian troops lay dead in the passes, and the massive Red armies ground ahead as fast as their supplies caught up with them. The brutal reality, the prime minister explained, had compelled him to shed his former illusions. "We were getting out of touch with the realities of the modern world. We were living in an atmosphere of our own creation."

But his statement and his country's subsequent actions revealed that he still had far to go in liberation from self-deception. He still considered the Soviet Union his friend and expected aid from it. And he still thought he could find safety in neutralism.

A month later, those hopes had faded only slightly. By December the Russian MIG fighter jets had not yet arrived. "We understand there has been some difficulty," the prime minister said, "but it has nothing to do with China." (Perhaps it did have; or perhaps the USSR wanted India to get in deeper.) Although the only help that reached the beleaguered Indians came from the West, they nonetheless evaded the painful reconsideration of past errors.

The experience of India had no perceptible impact upon the other uncommitted nations, which stubbornly clung to policies that threatened some day to expose them also to aggression. Indeed, in November there were efforts to draw Pakistan, theretofore a friend of the West, in the same direction. U Thant, recently elected secretary-general of the United Nations, called for a "spirit of compromise" with "give and take on both sides," as if the United States and the Soviet Union were equally prone to aggression.

As the year drew to a close, neutralism, the greatest illusion of all, persisted. Then and later, few commentators became aware either of its true meaning or of its disastrous effects upon the hopes for world order.

Its defenders often described neutralism as a policy of nonalignment adhered to by the new peace-loving Afro-Asian nations in order to further their own interests. Such a description was inaccurate on almost every count. Neutralism was partisan, European in origin, ideological in character, and a threat to the development of a rule of law that was the only hope for a durable peace.

The neutralism of the decades after 1945 was far removed from the traditional neutrality recognized in international law. Such states as Switzerland and Sweden adopted neutrality as a conscious policy out of unwillingness or inability to become involved in the nineteenth-century system of alliances. They did so because they were small, incapable of affecting the existing balance of power, and uninterested in expansion. They could therefore stand apart from the struggle for advantage that occupied the great nations.

However, those countries also accepted the peculiar obligations of their status. They understood that they had to be strong enough to defend themselves and free from dependence upon external support; otherwise their vulnerability might invite aggression and upset the balance of power. They also realized that they could aspire to no positive role in the normal play of international politics. Since they could only be bystanders to decisions that others made, their security rested upon a regime of international law. If they had not known it earlier, the experience of neutral Belgium in 1914 certainly enlightened them.

The neutralism of recent decades differed from traditional neutrality in every respect. It was a doctrine not of small but of great states, with populations as large as India's. Militarily weak and dependent upon foreign aid, the countries that adopted the policy of nonalignment nonetheless tried to constitute an independent force in international politics and, in doing so, generally (if unwittingly) threw their weight on the Soviet side. Lacking power, they could act only through appeals to reason and justice, which only the West respected.

Meanwhile, the Reds, contemptuous of weakness, operated without fear of restraint from this source.

These attitudes reached back to the immediate postwar years. Then, well before the countries that became the chief exponents of neutralism achieved independence, dissident Englishmen, Frenchmen, Germans, and Italians formulated the basic ideas of neutralism. They did so out of the need for giving intellectual respectability to the anti-Americanism to which socialist ideology bound them.

In England, France, and Italy a significant number of intellectuals and politicians had formed alliances with the Communists in the United Front before 1939. The betrayal of the Hitler-Stalin pact and the attack on Finland disillusioned some of them for a few years, but Russia's participation in the war reconstituted the antifascist collaboration, particularly in the resistance movements. That experience supplied the background against which most of the European non-Communist left interpreted the problems of the peace.

Harold J. Laski, Richard Crossman, and Aneurin Bevan in England, Jean-Paul Sartre and Claude Bourdet in France, Kurt Schumacher in Germany, and Pietro Nenni in Italy, among others, anticipated the development of some form of democratic socialism in their own countries; they considered neither the Soviet Union nor the United States a model worth emulating — the one reprehensible in its authoritarianism, the other in its capitalism. They would avoid both evils. At home they sought to oust the conservative parties and gradually to transfer ownership of the means of production to the state. In foreign policy, their salient objective was peace, to free energies for economic reconstruction.

From their point of view, both the United States and the

Soviet Union were threats: each stood ready to plunge the world into conflict that would destroy civilization to further its own view of the future — the one to spread Communism, the other to preserve capitalism. The superpowers, armed with terrible instruments of annihilation, prepared once more to make Europe a battleground; and the equal likelihood of danger from both sources created a moral parity between them.

For Europeans reluctant to be pushed to either extreme, salvation lay in the creation of a third force: the uncommitted countries advancing toward democratic socialism would hold together, throw their weight in whichever direction was necessary to establish an equilibrium, and thus neutralize disruptive tendencies from either the East or the West.

In the application of these abstract concepts to practice, however, there were significant differences between the judgments rendered of Soviet and American activities. The interpretation of Communist measures was consistently apologetic, while the United States was generally suspected of covert designs upon peace.

The European neutralists had had extensive experience in explaining away the peculiarities of the Soviet regime. They regarded the pact with Hitler as a lapse accounted for by the earlier transgressions of France and Britain at Munich. The disregard of solemn agreements in Eastern Europe after 1945 was necessary to ease Russian fears of attack from the West. The ruthless repressions of the Stalin era were either denied altogether as capitalist propaganda or mildly reproved as the inevitable incidents of a period of reconstruction. Jean-Paul Sartre, never a Party member, assured Frenchmen in 1954 that complete freedom of expression flourished in Russia; a socialist state could not really be anti-Semitic or send its people to slave-labor camps.

In any case, there was a disposition to minimize the importance of civil liberties; the well-known omelet could not be made without cracking some eggs. Besides, the United States was just as bad. Characteristically, Harold J. Laski's article on civil liberties in the Soviet Union in 1946 concluded with an attack on the private ownership of American newspapers.

With amazing gullibility, the neutralists accepted at face value Soviet professions of concern with peace and with the welfare of the working class everywhere. That a government in power for well over three decades required the use of terror to maintain itself aroused no disturbing questions in the minds of the neutralists of London and Paris. At the height of the Russian purges and the Ukrainian famine, Englishmen had read Sidney and Beatrice Webb's ecstatic 1936 account of Soviet democracy with approval; ten years later, at the height of Stalin's terror, they again placed their faith in the Red nirvana. Of course, they disapproved of censorship and of the police state, but not enough to shake their confidence in the beneficence of Communism. The system had improved the lot of the Russian people; it would do the same for the Czechs and the Poles. Meanwhile, all the peace lovers of the left could join in condemning the evils of British and French and American imperialism.

The events in Hungary in 1956 did not disturb the basic belief that Communism was only an extreme version of an acceptable leftist position — given to excess, no doubt, but nevertheless progressive in the light of history, which ordained development from the political democracy of capitalism to the economic democracy of socialism. The common Marxist rhetoric that many well-intentioned writers in Western Europe shared with the Reds persuaded them to accept verbal assurances that the Soviet Union labored toward the same objectives as they, and blinded them to the realities of Russian aggressiveness.

The neutralists' view of history also shaped their attitudes toward the United States. They believed that the capitalist stage in social evolution was drawing to a close as internal contradictions widened the gulf between the masses and the masters of wealth. The capitalists could block off the ascent to socialism only by finding other people to exploit or by repression. Imperialism provided the resources by which to appease the proletariat; fascism supplied the weapons by which to cling to control. Either course was a threat to peace.

The United States was the last stronghold of capitalism; its intentions, beneath the surface appearance of generosity, were essentially predatory. The aid it sent across the ocean was by no means disinterested, but designed to bring up to date an outmoded economic system, to inhibit the growth of a just social order, and ultimately to establish a permanent colonial relationship by which Europe would serve American interests. All those packages of food and crates of machinery were but means to diffuse a taste for Coca-Cola and breakfast cereals and to create a need for parts — a dependency that would add to the mounting profits of Yankee corporations whose greed would lead to disaster. American aid, wrote Laski in 1947, "would lay the foundation for capitalist revival on the continent; the capitalist revival would mean counter-revolution; that counter-revolution would mean civil war over half of Europe and perhaps more; and that civil war might very easily provoke a third world conflagration."

To the neutralists, the United States seemed to support unprogressive causes around the world. That in actuality it often took stands against colonialism that embarrassed its allies seemed less significant than the fact that it had long retained ties with Vichy France and made common cause with dictators in Nationalist China, Spain, and Portugal. It followed that the regimes it supported in Greece, Turkey, Poland, and Yugoslavia were also fascist in inclination. "The model all of us are approaching," explained *Le Combat,* is the police state. Moreover, unlike the Russians, who spoke as the champions of liberation everywhere, the Americans and their allies doggedly defended exploitative colonial empires throughout the world. Such was the version of world events many European neutralists accepted.

Anti-Americanism frequently swayed even conservatives who never drifted out of the orbit of the West. Bitter people who had suffered through the blitz or bombardment or German occupation scarcely concealed their resentment of a country that had remained thousands of miles away from the fighting. Proud people eagerly wished to believe that the gifts from across the Atlantic, on which they depended, were not the products of benevolence but of some ulterior selfish intention. Right-wing Tories in England, de Gaulle and some of his followers in France, and neofascists in Italy had reasons of their own for disliking the cultural influences that crossed the Atlantic, and they resented what they believed was the American part in depriving them of their empires. Whatever their sources, these emotions confirmed the neutralists in the habit of regarding every action of the United States with suspicion and strengthened the conviction that the two great powers were equally dangerous to peace.

The results were years of calamitous miscalculation. The Soviet Union maintained an immense force under arms and refused to consider any form of inspection that might limit atomic armaments. The United States promptly demobilized and formulated a scheme for the control of nuclear weapons, of which it had a monopoly until 1949. That did not alter the impression of American belligerence or of Russian conciliatory conduct. "If war begins between China and the United States," said *The New Statesman* in 1950, "the aggressor will not be the Communists." The light of the same curious logic distorted events in Greece, Czechoslovakia, and East Asia, the Marshall and Truman Plans, NATO, the Rosenberg case, and McCarthyism. "Yankee Go Home," scrawled across the walls of every European city, expressed the pervasive will to believe that if only the interlopers from the New World would halt their "phantom crusade against the U.S.S.R.," then the Old World would take care of its own affairs. That the genuine dangers came from the East was a fact that did not fit into the neutralists' image of the world, and was one, therefore, they resolutely refused to recognize.

Permanent residues of anti-Americanism remained in the language of even the moderate left, as when Pierre Elliott Trudeau in 1971 told an audience in Kiev that Canada befriended Russia to counter the United States threat "to our identity, from the cultural, economic and perhaps even military point of view." But the neutralists never won power in any Western European country during the 1950s and 1960s. Even in the Labor and Social Democratic parties in which their greatest strength lay, they were a minority — useful in criticizing enemies of the center and right, but never approaching office nor ever in a position to shape policy. When American aid stimulated economic recovery and growth, their popular following dwindled, not to revive until the 1970s. The rising standard of living enabled Europeans to form their own conclusions about the relative merits of their own system and of Communism. A hard core of committed Party members remained sympathizers of the Soviet Union; others perceived that the free world could find safety only in common action. After 1950 it no longer seemed plausible to argue, as a correspondent of *The New Statesman* did, that while the North Koreans had been guilty of aggression, they were not to be resisted, because the result would be "restoration of corrupt and oppressive oligarchies which happened to suit American capitalism." The exposure of the Stalinist dictatorship and of Soviet brutality in Hungary and Czechoslovakia further discredited neutralism.

Anti-Americanism, until revived by the New Left during the 1960s, lingered in Europe as a prejudice of aging intellectuals trapped by the commitment to old ideas. However much they praised the Red Chinese or made a hero of Castro, their influence waned. As an effective political program in Europe, neutralism was dead in the two decades after 1950 (except in Yugoslavia, where it justified Tito's maverick line.)

The concept flourished in Asia and Africa, however. India, Ghana, Egypt, Burma, and many other countries that acquired their independence after World War II proved remarkably receptive to the idea. The nationalist movements in Morocco, Algeria, Egypt, India, Indonesia, and elsewhere had fought the allies of the United States — England, France, Belgium, the Netherlands, and Portugal. In the course of the struggle, the colonial oppressors blurred into a single conglomerate target, the hateful image of which endured long after independence. By contrast, the Soviet Union appeared free of the taint of imperialism and loudly supported liberation.

The colonial heritage thus contributed an anti-Western orientation to the new nations, which entirely forgot the gains from earlier European contacts and converted the imperialist past into a record of unmitigated exploitation. Concessions, when they came, were taken as signs not of democracy, but of weakness. The contrast between the American treatment of the Philippines (or the British withdrawal from Africa) and the Soviet control over its satellites did not seem relevant to the rulers of Ceylon or India. The imperialism issue, formulated before 1939, overshadowed every other consideration and planted an anti-Western bias in countries that achieved independence in the 1950s and 1960s.

The question of color added an emotional pitch to attitudes in the newly liberated parts of the world. A few tardy gestures of conciliation could not excise the shameful pages in the record of the contacts of whites with the yellow and black peoples of Asia and Africa. The accumulated resentments of generations now fanned the emerging nations' smoldering hate toward the former master races. And the fact that the new states still needed technical material aid added to their bitterness. Pride demanded that they receive help not with gratitude but with condescension, as an obligation due them. They had a long account to settle with the whites of the West. The predisposition to hostility sensitized the Asians, and even more so the Africans, to race relations in the United States. The slow evolution toward equality that marked desegregation there reminded many Nigerians and Ghanaians of inequality, of the degradation of slavery, of the former masters in their clubs denying the humanity of the Kaffir. Washington and Pretoria fused as centers from which whites exploited blacks.

Control of the new governments fell into the hands of an educated minority isolated from the whole society. Ideologically, the bureaucrats insisted that the peasants and workers were the country's progressive force, yet by no means wished to identify with the masses in mode of life. The servants of the people knew the immense difficulties in the way of raising the general standards of material existence, yet were unwilling to wait for decent homes or for tastes of personal pleasure until enough was available for everyone. Indirect rewards rarely sufficed.

Most of the leaders of the new nations were socialists by commitment; and the struggle for freedom confirmed their deep-rooted distrust of the Wall Street capitalists who they thought controlled Western governments. Consequently, the Soviet Union was exempt from the general opprobrium attached to Europeans; a general article of faith informed neutralists that prejudice was a phenomenon of capitalism and that a socialist society was free of that evil.

Before independence Kwame Nkrumah, Krishna Menon, Nehru, and a good many other future leaders of the Asian and African countries had spent time in London and Paris as students or as exiles; they had become involved in the left intellectual circles most sympathetic to their aspirations for freedom. Laski, *The New Statesman,* and the ideologists of the United Front — their mentors — imbued them with the conviction that the causes of liberty and of socialism were identical. Interpreting the world in terms of the class struggle, the future leaders went back to their countries convinced that imperialism was the instrument by which the capitalist rulers of the West kept them enslaved. At home they found evidence to support that conclusion. Although the radicals sometimes enlisted the aid of middle-class nationalists, as in Egypt and India, the indigenous men of wealth usually worked hand in glove with the colonial authorities, thus confirming the impression that a social revolution was necessary to complete the political one. At independence the former ruling classes, if not liquidated, fled into exile, leaving in office influential native and European bureaucrats and advisers with strong leftist orientations.

In some places the paucity of informed personnel magnified neutralist influences. British and French efforts to train officials qualified to take power had fallen far short of the need, and other regimes had been even more derelict in this respect. The responsibility for critical decisions about foreign policy therefore often devolved upon people inadequately acquainted with any but their own immediate problems.

Their socialist governments believed that they could achieve rapid economic development, their first requirement, only through public ownership and centralized planning. The experience of the West was irrelevant, while the Communist nations offered them models worth emulating. Uncritically accepting as accurate fantastic claims of Russian and Chinese "great leaps forward" and dismissing the evidence of Western Europe, Nasser, Nkrumah, and Sukarno callously risked disorder in the existing economy and a decline of the standard of living in the interest of forced industrialization. Freedom, for the neutralists, therefore had a simple meaning — freedom from white colonial rule. Their European teachers had taught them to devalue the importance of civil rights; and the exigencies of establishing control made the new regimes in Ghana and Indonesia, and elsewhere, fully as repressive as the British or Dutch had been. Warnings about the dangers of Red totalitarianism failed to impress Nkrumah or Sukarno. "Telling Ghanaians to beware of Communists," said the former in 1960, "is like telling a man in a burning house not to go outside because it may start to snow."

Previously unsuspected features of independence added passion to neutralism. The new states, with boundaries set by Europeans, proved to embrace peoples divided by religion, tribe, ethnicity, and language — peoples once united by hostility to colonial masters, now ever on the edge of fragmentation. Unity required establishment of a national identity. When the collapse of ancient institutions lowered the value of human life, there seemed one alternative to despair: somehow to satisfy the desire for dignity and meaning through the all-comprehending entity of the nation. Again and again stoked-up nationalism compensated for intolerable social deficiencies, enabling men and women to explain the difficulties of the present by the past sins of outsiders. The West was vulnerable to criticism not only for past faults but also because it remained the source from which disruptive cultural and social influences still radiated. And most vulnerable was the United States, the most Western and long the most affluent.

The withdrawal of Western influences from the less developed portions of the earth left behind an institutional shambles. The traditional modes of control collapsed; the few intellectuals clutched at vague, unassimilated ideologies; the bureaucracies were unskilled; and the population was bewildered. Never mind the extravagant eccentricities of Idi Amin, Colonel Moammar Khadafy, or the Ayatollah Khomeini! Never mind the Latin American dictators of the right or left. Consider the neutralist nationalism of Juan Bosch, a man of evident sincerity and of unimpeachable integrity, a confirmed democrat and the first constitutional president of the Dominican Republic after the long nightmare of Trujillo dictatorship. Here was his "plan of action," while president, for coping with a threat from Haiti: the Dominican army was to mobilize on the border close to Haiti's capital, and the air force would fly over Port-au-Prince warning the people to flee before the bombs fell. If absolutely essential, two or three bombs would be dropped where they would cause no casualties. No more would be necessary because Haiti's president would thereupon resign. "But the plan had one flaw,"

Bosch wrote. "I could confide it to no one, not even the military commanders who would participate in it." Such fancies were the products of a mind distorted by nationalism and unequipped to deal with the problems of a country in torment. National pride, Bosch explained, reached far back to his childhood. "No one will ever know what my seven-year-old soul suffered at the sight" of the Dominican flag lowered during the protectorate. "This caused me indescribable pain, and even kept me awake a long time after I had been sent to bed."

Nationalism reinforced neutralism. These regimes refused formally to commit themselves on cold-war issues. They did not wish to adopt or to favor either capitalism or Communism, systems they identified respectively with the United States and the Soviet Union. Instead they were to constitute a middle group pursuing an independent policy, vigilantly on guard against threats to peace equally likely to come from the West as from the East. They were to supply a vehicle for possible negotiations between the two great power blocs. In practice that meant that the neutrals, refusing to make a moral judgment between the two antagonists, usually tried to compromise with, rather than resist, the aggressors; and the more intransigent one party was in a dispute, the more pressure fell on the other to yield in order to arrive at an accommodation. The neutralists' course was thus inconsistent with collective security and with the orderly development of international law.

On concrete issues the neutralists swung invariably into the Russian orbit, because the Communists never made any secret of their views. Long before they enunciated the Brezhnev doctrine to explain the invasion of Czechoslovakia, they had made their internationalist duty clear. Following both Lenin's injunction back in 1915 that a socialist state bore the duty of helping the oppressed classes of other countries and the lesson of nonintervention in the Spanish Civil War, they insisted that they would act wherever feasible. In every confrontation, therefore, the neutrals knew that only a Western retreat would preserve peace.

The first steps toward formation of a bloc came at the Asian Relations Conferences held in 1947 and 1949 at New Delhi, shortly after Indian independence. Events in Palestine and Korea thereafter persuaded the Arab and Asian countries to work together in the United Nations. They did not thereby become a single cohesive unit, but divided on issues that affected their immediate interests, as in the rivalry between Egypt and the other Arab states. And the West found occasional friends in the area between Tunisia and the Philippines. But it could not slow the general tendency toward neutralism in the conflicts stirred up by Communist aggression.

The decisive steps came in 1954. The settlements in Geneva that year temporarily brought to a halt the aggression supported by China in Korea and Indochina; Chou En-lai then agreed with the prime ministers of India and Burma upon the five principles of peaceful coexistence; and President Sukarno of Indonesia summoned a meeting the next year in Bandung to define the contribution the peoples of Asia and Africa could "make to the promotion of world peace and cooperation."

The invitations were deliberately selective — to the Arab states, but not to Israel; to the central African federation, but not to South Africa; to the People's Republic of China, but not to the Chinese Republic; to the Gold Coast, but not to Nigeria. That is, nations with a Western orientation were excluded. From the session emerged ten flawless principles of justice and international cooperation, affirming respect for fundamental human rights, racial equality, abstention from interference in other countries, renunciation of "acts or threats of aggression or the use of force," and the right of all colonies to independence. The conference also called upon the great powers to suspend the production or testing of all nuclear weapons. Subsequent consultations and continuing collaboration in the United Nations attempted to preserve unity of action toward those desirable goals.

In the spirit of those principles, the neutrals the next year joined in condemning the Anglo-French-Israeli aggression in Suez. With their help, and that of the United States, the United Nations secured a withdrawal of the invading forces. It was in that spirit, too, that most of the neutrals voted for the admission of Red China to the United Nations, supported the regime of Patrice Lumumba and denounced Belgian activities in the Congo, welcomed the grant of independence to one African state after another, and hailed the suspension of atomic testing in 1959. All these measures, whatever their intrinsic merits, were adverse to the West.

From the 1973 Algiers summit meeting onward, neutralist attention shifted to economic issues, with the West still culpable. The nonaligned states found nothing relevant in the development and land reform of Korea, Hong Kong, Malaya, Singapore, Taiwan, and the Philippines. Instead they called for a massive transfer of resources from the rich (Western) regions to their own; and the UN General Assembly in 1974 and 1975 promptly agreed.

Not once did the neutrals take an equally strong stand on the far clearer Communist violations of the Bandung principles. With what cynicism Chou acceded to those pleasant propositions, we can well imagine; he had already been guilty of aggression in Korea and had supplied much of the weaponry that won the war against France in Indochina. Those misdemeanors did not cool the warmth of his reception at the conference. Thereafter, the brutal repression of all human rights in North Vietnam and in China itself, the march into Tibet and the persecution of its people, and the shelling of Quemoy and Matsu earned not the slightest reproof. The neutralists explained these actions away as steps by which a progressive regime protected itself. Even frequent violations of India's frontiers evoked no strictures from Nehru's friends, and the open attack in October 1962 brought offers of mediation rather than condemnation of the aggressor. The fighting in the Himalayas was inadequate to prove the belligerence of Communism.

The Soviet Union fared equally well. In the same month as the events in Suez, Soviet troops invaded Hungary against the will of the legitimate government of that country. No effective response followed an appeal to the United Nations. India and Yugoslavia particularly distinguished themselves in evading responsibility for the principles they professed. Tito's legation in Budapest callously turned over the fugitives who found refuge within its walls to their assassins; and the Indian representative in the United Nations occupied himself in quest of a solution to please the Russians.

The uncommitted countries consistently accepted as evidence of his pacific intentions Khrushchev's call for immediate total disarmament, overlooking the roadblocks he repeatedly threw up in the way of practical steps toward that end. By the same token, the Soviet use of the veto in the UN Security Council and Soviet disregard of the recommendations of the General Assembly did not seem to run counter to the respect for world opinion the neutrals demanded of the West. Nor did the people of Berlin seem entitled to the right to self-determination; as Tito explained in 1960, "peaceful coexistence could not halt the historical processes in international life."

The resumption of nuclear testing in 1961 revealed the double standard that exempted the Communists from the criteria by which the West was judged. Asian students in August of that year felt strongly about the bomb and agreed that renewal of explosions that polluted the world's atmosphere would be a crime against humanity; they assumed, however, that violations of the ban would come from the United States. The Soviet Union could not conceivably take a step that would damage the common man everywhere. Nonetheless, news that the Russians had indeed resumed testing only slightly perturbed neutrals who immediately came around to the explanation that Khrushchev must have acted to anticipate an American resumption he knew was coming. By the time the conference of neutrals met in Belgrade, evidence of Soviet perfidy was clear. The delegates hemmed and hawed at the violation of a crucial Bandung principle, and in the end issued a call to both the United States and Russia to refrain from testing, as if both were equally culpable. In November a statement by Krishna Menon, then foreign minister of India, ascribed the ultimate blame to the Americans. He and his colleagues had closed their minds to the possibility that a Communist state could be guilty of misdeeds that their prejudices informed them were always committed by capitalists.

Nor did the neutrals take the Bandung principles as limitations upon their own freedom of action. The obligations to respect the right to self-determination and to refrain from the threats to use force applied to the wicked imperialists. But India felt no compunction about refusing to accede to the plebiscite in Kashmir suggested by the United Nations and it ruthlessly moved its army into Goa, a province that had been Portuguese for more than four centuries. Indonesia's actions in western Irian and Egypt's in Yemen showed the same unscrupulous disregard for a moral code they sanctimoniously urged upon others. In the light of Marxist history, a progressive state could do no wrong.

Nor did the neutrals learn anything at all from the experience of the eighteen years after 1962. India simply evaded its responsibilities as chairman of the International Control Commission in Indochina, and unhesitatingly made war on Pakistan when it was to its advantage. It called for recognition of the Palestine Liberation Organization but would not recognize Israel; and it refused to permit inspection to determine the use made of atomic fuel exported to it. The Soviet invasion of Czechoslovakia disturbed not one of the neutrals. Nor did any show concern about the raging war on the horn of Africa. Significantly, in September 1980, when Iraq invaded Iran, the neutral intermediaries worked for a cease-fire that would reward the aggressor.

The only departures from neutralism occurred in Southeast Asia, primarily as a result of the American stand in the Vietnamese War. The displacement of Sukarno and the massacre of hundreds of thousands of overseas Chinese shifted Indonesia into the Western camp; and Singapore, Malaya, and Thailand were close enough to events to have no illusions about the meaning of neutrality.

The revival of neutralism in areas remote from the scene of immediate fighting offset those gains. The New Left of the 1960s, detached enough to harbor illusions and swayed by utopianism, easily transferred its loyalty from Stalin to his successors and from them to Mao or the Albanians. Anything was possible if only willed enough. In the face of the destruction of Czech reform efforts, the New Left still talked of socialism with a human face and clung to the bogey of the American threat. Refuge in that antique position was more comfortable than confrontation with harsh realities.

The growth of Soviet power drove some conservatives in the same direction. De Gaulle led the way for the French, partly out of brutal calculation, for geography provided France with a NATO shield in Germany. Pique and personal resentment against the Anglo-Saxons contributed to de Gaulle's neutralism, which led to effective withdrawal from NATO and to reliance upon a dangerous national nuclear force and upon an erratic and self-centered foreign policy. Finlandization in the 1970s became an attractive alternative to collective security. That little country had to accept the suzerainty of its powerful neighbor, along with drastic limitations upon its internal freedom and upon its foreign relations. The prospect of doing the same seemed tolerable for those reluctant to face the difficult alternative. Denmark and other NATO countries backed away from their defense commitments; talk about an opening to the East spread in Germany and Norway; and the British Labour party conference of May 31, 1980, moved well along in the same direction.

In the West as in the East, the calculation of immediate costs made the position of bystander increasingly attractive. In the long run, of course, the aggressor might turn upon the bystander also. But for the moment the comforting pretense that both parties to any quarrel were at fault rendered aloofness comfortable. So, the three socialist neutrals who went to Tehran to investigate the American hostages returned reassured. Bruno Kreisky, Felipe González, and Olof Palme discovered that really "36 million Iranians" were "prisoners of the hostages" and asked the United States to release the Iranian funds it had frozen.

Meanwhile, neutralism had helped destroy collective security. In foreign policy all nations, large and small, had one clear and vital interest: the preservation of peace and the nurture of a system of international law that alone would protect them against interference and insure them the freedom to devote their energy to their own development. The neutrals served that interest badly.

From the calamities of the greatest war theretofore fought, few consolations emerged other than the hope of avoiding a repetition of the disaster. That feeble glimmer lighted the way to the United Nations, a body some believed might lead to a world order within which states would learn to deal with one another through reason and law rather than through violence.

All that was a dream, perhaps, but one worth cherishing. The uncommitted nations might have brought it a little closer to reality had they been genuinely neutral and applied the same moral criteria in every conflict. They did not. They fell in with the game of power politics, seeking what they could for themselves; and they played the role of brokers between East and West, expecting each side to yield a little, regardless of justice — partitions in Korea and Indochina, coalition in Laos, the cession of Guantanamo in return for the Russian missile bases. In the process, all questions of principles receded conveniently into the background, and the uncompromising extremists, willing to risk conflict, gained an advantage over those committed to a reasonable, peaceful adjustment of differences.

The neutralists, blind to the genuine source of danger after 1945, allowed past grievances against the white capitalists of the West to conceal the greater threat from the

East. Visions of idyllic socialism obscured what Communism had actually become — the militant doctrine of totalitarian regimes with expansive urges. Statesmen who refused to look candidly at the forces about them were in no position to help bring order to a disordered world.

5

A Note on Legality

A BRIEF NOTE PROVIDES sufficient epitaph for postwar hopes of international legality.

The hope that law would regulate the relations of states as it did that of individuals long antedated the concept of collective security. It was a matter of mere prudence that sovereign powers in their dealings with one another adhere to agreed-upon rules lest they otherwise constantly engage in damaging conflicts. Realism demanded that they keep their guard up and risk a fight only when there was a clear advantage to doing so; and preparedness inhibited potential outbreaks of violence.

Precepts that dated back to the middle ages encouraged adherence to the rules. Catholic teachings described the Christian conduct of a just war; and chivalry dictated proper behavior even against infidel Moors. True, practice often degenerated in bloody spurts of cruelty, but that did not lessen the attractiveness of the ideal, to which the treatises of Hugo Grotius and Emmerich von Vattel gave formal expression. Eighteenth-century diplomacy began to exemplify in practice the proper conduct of members of the family of nations; and the Concert of Europe after 1815 attempted to impose those regulations not only within the Continent, but around the world. The suppression of piracy and of the slave trade were monuments of success in striving toward those goals.

Hence the shock after 1945 at deviations from the rules. Certainly the great war just ended had shown the ease of relapse to barbarism; and the trials at Nuremberg and elsewhere had attempted to define war crimes.

But the lessons of the past were lost on the generation that grew to maturity after the peace. Attacks on unarmed civilians by guerrillas became commonplace and the seizure of ambassadors followed. Although governments at first frowned on such incidents, in time some of them actually approved. In 1973 no one openly defended the murder of the United States envoy to the Sudan; a few years later Russian advisers directed the Afghans responsible for the assassination of the American ambassador in Kabul. In 1979 Iran justified the occupation of the American embassy and imprisonment of its personnel as hostages while all the blunt instruments of international law proved of no assistance whatever. It was by then vain to look to the United Nations for legislation or to expect that the rulings of the International Court of Justice would command respect.

The deterioration was not the work only of the ideological foes of the West or of people divided from it by vast cultural differences. Even liberal, democratic states, lacking confidence in the efficacy of law and despairing of any other solutions, drifted into action contrary to international law without counting the consequences. Pleas of national interest or survival were paramount. Turkish troops invaded Cyprus when provoked by a unilateral change in the status of that island by Archbishop Makarios. Several countries of their own accord expanded their territorial waters from the previously recognized three miles to two hundred miles, whatever the consequences for others. Ecuador seized American tuna boats venturing beyond the line it drew; and Iceland went to the verge of war against Britain to extend its control over the fisheries it considered necessary for its livelihood. In 1979 China invaded Vietnam, which had overrun Cambodia; and in 1980 Iraq attacked Iran with total unconcern for legality.

Every citizen has a stake in prosecuting criminals who break the law, because each is a potential future victim. But when confidence in the system of justice fades, each prudently seeks personal protection or falls back on vigilante action. In the same situation, when justice fails, states, like individuals, disregard laws, either because they do not recognize their legitimacy; or because of deliberate calculations of advantage; or because of passion, hatred, or ignorance.

Turkey, Iceland, and Ecuador did not wish to destroy international law; indeed, in other circumstances, they claimed its protection. They sought only this once to bend away its inconveniences, and reserved to themselves the right to judge the necessity of doing so. Since every nation claimed the same right and repeatedly exercised it, the number of exceptions soon obliterated the general rule. Still, in the absence of a binding general law, sovereign states put their own vital interests first.

Idi Amin suffered no punishment when he gratuitously humiliated a foreign diplomat. But the issue was clear: opinion throughout the world considered the act wrong, though nothing could be done to halt its repetition. The most difficult cases involved genuine grievances that drove a state to act in contravention of accepted law. In 1976 an elite brigade of Israeli armed forces landed at Entebbe in Uganda, seized the international airport, liberated almost all the hostages held in a hijacked Air France plane, and returned to Tel Aviv.

The whole operation was illegal. The attackers invaded the territory of a sovereign state, fired upon its troops, and caused considerable property damage. Yet the incident earned no more than a ripple of criticism and almost everywhere aroused admiration for the skill of its planning and the courage of its execution.

The raid hardly required justification. Idi Amin, Uganda's ruler, had already acquired a dubious reputation for disregard of international niceties and was guilty of the far greater crime of sheltering the hijackers. Moreover, the innocent hostages faced unpredictable dangers, and the urgency of the crisis prevented time-consuming diplomatic or judicial appeals. Then too, the raid succeeded, doing relatively little harm either to Entebbe or to the principles of international law.

The issues had been even more complex in May 1960 when an arm of the Israeli secret service tracked down a Nazi fugitive in Argentina and abducted him to stand trial in Jerusalem before a court that condemned him to death. Argentina was not Uganda, nor was the case for urgency so strong as to exclude alternative procedures. The government of Israel, in its exchange of notes with Argentina, in effect admitted that the seizure of Adolf Eichmann lacked legality; and that certainly was the tenor of the United Nations resolution on the matter. The Argentine protests, however, were only a formality; no government cared enough about Eichmann to come to his defense. Yet violation of the rights of even the worst of criminals had serious repercussions.

Israel claimed jurisdiction on the grounds that it spoke for the Jewish people who were Eichmann's victims (although it acknowledged that Gypsies and Slavs, among others, were also destined for enslavement or extermination) and that justice demanded the punishment of all those responsible for the crimes of the concentration camps, because all humanity was the victim. But Israel did not concede that the trial, conviction, and condemnation in a sense did not go beyond satisfaction of private grievances since justice was not done according to appropriate procedures.

"Had Eichmann been tried by an international court," the *St. Louis Post-Dispatch* said, "the verdict probably would not have been different. Yet that decision would have been made by an independent judiciary speaking for the conscience of all humanity." Alas, in 1961 there was no such court. It had been the great achievement of the Nuremberg trials, Telford Taylor explained, to have operated not simply as the instrument of powerful victors against a defeated enemy, but as an international tribunal seeking to define a rule of law. Israel departed from this pattern. Little more than a decade had passed since those trials; and the likelihood of constituting a similar court had all but vanished. The Soviet Union no longer cooperated in such efforts, not the least because of the revelations about its own system of justice and the crimes of its own leaders.

Claiming full competence to judge its own jurisdiction and procedures, Israel therefore accused the Nazi not of crimes against humanity but of crimes against Jews — and thus set particular interests apart from the more general, universal ones.

Eichmann's seizure also sacrificed the principle of the right of refuge. For more than a century people interested in freedom had argued that fugitives could be seized only by a legal process and only for crimes personally committed. The right of asylum assumed that there were limits to the power of the state, which could not act outside the jurisdiction in which prescription or the consent of the governed gave it authority. In January 1968 the government of India went the whole way. It requested embassies in Delhi to bar political refugees, after a member of the Soviet youth delegation fled to the American mission.

The Eichmann trial and its aftermath supplied an ironic commentary on the efforts of those who had fought against fascism to develop an international rule of law to prevent repetition of the barbarities they had survived.

The Nazi himself died as he had lived — without the least understanding of his crime; and the trial elicited nothing not already known about the catastrophe. That Eichmann was guilty of something and that his actions were evil were beyond doubt. The crucial questions were, however, how to define the nature of the guilt and how to understand the character of the evil. Eichmann was far from the initiator of the "final solution" to the Jewish problem under the Third Reich. This bureaucrat implemented policies formulated by others. An ordinary man, doing a job like everyone else, obedient and anxious to further his career, he signed papers, pushed buttons, spoke on the telephone, made calculations, and arranged schedules — the usual tasks of civilized life. Only the result was a monstrous crime.

Hitler and the Nazi party leaders were, in the first instance, responsible for the catastrophe. But complicity spread throughout the society they dominated. The lines of command reached downward from Hitler's chancellery to the manipulator of the gas chamber valve, passing through the whole society and tainting all who collaborated or simply stood by. Every branch of the German government had a hand in implementing the policy, and every German was implicated, directly or indirectly. The rulers and the people of the conquered territories either stood by or lent a hand. The United States and its allies failed to intervene or to provide a refuge. Only those like Anton Schmidt, a German sergeant executed for aiding the Jews, escaped a share of the guilt. But such instances were pitifully few. Totalitarian domination dragged down into the same mire all whom it touched, for it posed a general dilemma for men and women who valued order and rationality. Guilt was whole and continuous, embracing all.

Many obeyed. Some were more guilty than others. Why? The narrow grounds taken in the Eichmann trial did not further the development of an international penal code that would have attempted a valid definition of a crime against humanity. Nor did events in the subsequent decades supply an answer.

The Nuremberg trials were more creative, for they defined as crimes against humanity acts that were themselves inhuman, whoever the victims. But people were less likely to value the distinction in 1961 than a decade earlier, and were even less likely to do so a decade later. Experience should have persuaded the world of the absolute urgency of developing an international code to limit the immoral use of sovereign state power. Instead, the failure of the peace heightened nationalism and produced a strident insistence that each state regulate its own conduct. In a world perilous beyond any earlier imagining, safety rested in the intimate group, and the very concept of general humanity grew vague and indistinct.

The regrets are not for Eichmann but for the faded concept of a governing law. His case was not critical; it did not account for, but was symptomatic of, the general abandonment of hope in an international order — an abandonment that events in the 1960s and 1970s would amplify. Violence spread to satisfy national, tribal, and ideological urges; terrorism — easy, atavistic — became an end in itself; and the value of human life dwindled. Susan Atkins of the Manson family felt a form of sexual release when she stabbed away; the "people of the free universe" executed five who misused "the natural environment"; the PLO and the Irish Republican Army each waged holy war; Panthers and guerrillas prowled the cities; and fanatical or cynical governments for reasons of their own dispatched limitless supplies to hands willing to use them.

By 1980 *moralism* had become a term of reproach among sophisticated American commentators — "camouflage that reeked of idealism," according to the editor of *Daedalus*. Vestiges of the hope that ethical considerations would extend to foreign affairs lingered in the legal requirements of an annual State Department report on human rights in countries receiving aid, in the text of the Helsinki accords, and in the Jackson-Vanik Amendment. But in the absence of any standards, fluffy pronouncements about human rights floated off into profound ambiguities and contradictions. In March 1977 President Carter spoke of the need for a "Palestinian homeland." Why not one for the Kurds or Armenians or, for that matter, the Basques or the Corsicans?

In the beleaguered Warsaw ghetto, the archivist Emmanuel Ringelblum noted that everyone was keeping diaries: "journalists and writers, of course, but also teachers, public men, young people — even children." In those last desperate moments of fading hope they clung to the wish that a memorial would survive from which "the historian of the future" might draw some meaning. Let the wasteful sacrifices of their times at least inform the understanding of posterity. Forty years had passed after the Holocaust swept across Europe in 1939. From the rage for destruction that took millions of lives, from the havoc wrought by marching armies and aerial armadas, the survivors learned little.

6

Vietnam

VIETNAM IS THE HIDDEN ULCER in the American consciousness. Military defeat and bitter internal dissension banished discussion of that event from political discourse after the end of United States involvement. The politicians, the people, and the analysts have until recently conveniently drawn a blanket of silence over the whole episode.

Yet Vietnam did happen and brought to a head the great crisis of twentieth-century diplomacy. It became an ineradicable part of the American past. Those who would not repeat errors must understand them. Without the willingness to confront the actuality of the disaster, as it happened, the nation runs the risk that the hidden ulcer will bleed it to death.

Vietnam was the end result of a foreign policy developed in the decades after 1945 under the administrations of Presidents Truman, Eisenhower, Kennedy, and Johnson. That policy was defensive; in order to minimize the risks of nuclear war, it aimed to create conditions of international stability by resisting aggression, whether overt or under the cover of subversion. In a divided world, armed forces confronting one another across uncertain boundaries would frequently clash. The task of statesmanship was to keep those incidents to a minimum, and to contain them by resisting with only enough force to inhibit further aggression. The defensive policy ran counter to the basic military tradition of the United States. Like MacArthur, Generals Marshall, Pershing, and Grant, and Presidents Franklin D. Roosevelt, Wilson, and Lincoln all believed that war was hell and that the only way to get it over with was to mobilize maximum power and destroy the enemy.

After 1950 the United States departed from the tradition when it recognized that it could no longer destroy the enemy without destroying itself. The alternative to nuclear warfare was graduated deterrence; the response to provocation was to take one step at a time, escalating the scale of combat only as much as necessary to repulse the antagonist, but also meeting each blow with pain-inflicting retaliation.

The success of the defensive posture depended upon two corollaries. First, the United States would match any escalation in the level of conflict so that firmness would demonstrate the hazards of the resort to violence, and yet would do so without the overreaction that might raise the level of force employed. Second, the defensive posture required surrendering to the aggressor the choice of the time and place of conflict. The United States and its allies could not take the initiative or attack where the enemy was weakest, but had to allow the enemy to choose the battlefield, remaining prepared to shift from one area of defense to another at the convenience of the aggressor. When peace came to Korea in 1953, President Eisenhower understood that the next attack would come in Southeast Asia. Yet, having rejected General MacArthur's plan for total war to destroy Asian Communism, the United States could do perilously little other than wait to ward off the next blow. Vietnam followed.

The only alternative open to Eisenhower, Kennedy, and Johnson was reversion to the old strategy, rejected when Truman forced MacArthur to resign. But without graduated, step-by-step resistance, massive nuclear retaliation was the sole response to aggression.

The following factual statements, put as simply and concisely as possible, will help correct frequent misstatements of the issues.

Until the 1950s the United States had no stake of any consequence in Southeast Asia. It did not desire the restoration of French rule in Indochina any more than it wished the Dutch returned to Indonesia. It favored no particular regime and was, at first, perfectly willing to contemplate a government under Ho Chi Minh. In the immediate postwar years, however, this was not a pressing issue, because Communists participated in the French government and did not object to having the earlier connection reestablished. When the United Front collapsed, the French sought to regain control of Indonesia, using American aid to do so. But the United States did not become directly involved, not even after Communist victory in China in 1949 opened a flow of supplies from the north, not even after the French disaster at Dien Bien Phu.

The effort to make peace at Geneva in 1954 produced a complex of agreements — to regulate the status of Cambodia, to provide a settlement for Laos, and to draw across Vietnam a line separating two distinct, internationally recognized governments. That division had the same validity as that in Korea or in Germany. Furthermore, it recognized existing cultural and social differences in an area occupied by Westernized and traditional folk, by Roman Catholics, Buddhists, Taoists, and Confucians, by adherents of the Cao

Dai and Hoa Hao sects, by Montagnard tribesmen, and by about a million "overseas" Chinese.

In the ancient past a single unified government had ruled Vietnam at some times but not at others. Before the Japanese invasion it had consisted of three separate states — Tonkin and Annam, under a French protectorate, and Cochin China, a colony. There was no more reason to unite them than East and West Germany or North and South Korea or for that matter Germany and Austria. At Geneva the parties divided hopelessly over unification and never did agree. In the final statement closing the conference, the British chairman expressed the hope that free elections would allow the people of Vietnam to make a choice within two years after the signature; and that statement entered into the record. The American observer said that the United States would not oppose such a solution. But the Saigon government never agreed.

In any case a North Vietnamese reign of terror soon made the issue of elections hopelessly academic. The Lao Dong, or Communist party, controlled all the key positions and broke all agreements; as Senator John F. Kennedy explained, "an election obviously stacked and subverted in advance" would be meaningless. The mass flight of almost a million refugees across the border to the South showed what the people thought of the choice available to them.

The Geneva agreements brought no peace to the peninsula. The hope for coalition government in Laos proved vain and a long period of warfare across ill-defined borders lasted for twenty years, for the Pathet Lao enjoyed North Vietnamese, Russian, and Chinese support. Gradually, but inadequately, the United States assisted the recognized government and might have drawn the line there. Instead it accepted a cease-fire and compromise on July 23, 1962, in return for the Soviet Union undertaking to guarantee the provision against use of Laos for the transit of materials or men into South Vietnam. Hanoi never honored the agreement; nor did Moscow act to secure compliance; nor did the United States protest effectively.

The opening of the Ho Chi Minh Trail led to more serious violations in Vietnam, in a familiar combination of subversion through the Viet Cong and invasion across the border. The response by the United States, matching the escalation in aggression, culminated in 1964 in the Gulf of Tonkin Resolution and the widening of the war. Later, critics incorrectly asserted that the senators who voted for the Gulf of Tonkin Resolution did not intend to grant sweeping powers to President Johnson. The evidence belies the assertion. The two senators who voted in the negative fully explained the consequences of the resolution; and the earnestness of the debates made the meaning clear. In sponsoring the resolution, Senator J. William Fulbright explained that the North Vietnamese regime was "patently guilty of military aggression and demonstrably in contempt of international law." The new type of war, "a modernized, specialized kind of aggression" was "just as savage and as much in violation of international good behavior" as the overt invasion by troops. The resolution would not limit the president's power to land a large American army in Vietnam or in China, but authorized the commander in chief to do whatever he thought necessary.

No doubt the senator later regretted his words. At the time, he, like the president, hoped that a firm statement of the American position would induce the North Vietnamese to slow their attack on the South. But the Senate explicitly canvassed the possibility that the resolution might not have the desired inhibiting effect and that it might lead to the dispatch of ground troops, to the bombing of Hanoi, and to the intervention of Red China.

As the fighting in Vietnam intensified, so did the war of words at home. No other military enterprise, once launched, evoked such dissent in the United States. The sustained debate reflected the uncertainty of a nation moving along a course for which history had ill prepared it. In this conflict there could be no illusions about an early total victory or any easy way out. The British had needed 400,000 armed men and eleven years to protect Malaya against 15,000 guerrillas; and it had taken almost as much effort to put down the Huks in the Philippines. Yet President Kennedy hoped in 1962 that 5,000 marines would turn the tide. Patience was the quality Americans were least likely to display; hence, the deepening mood of frustration.

The debate during the 1960s rarely considered seriously the genuine alternatives to administration policy: rapid, decisive escalation, with all its risks; or complete withdrawal, with all its penalties. The discussion that was not purely defensive of administration policy drifted toward wishful thinking: if only somehow the United States would try hard enough, or if South Vietnamese President Ngo Dinh Diem or the generals would reform, then peace would be there for the asking. Any hopeful hint from a Hungarian or Rumanian official possibly in touch with Hanoi touched off waves of speculations, rounds of diplomatic activity, and hopeful thoughts about mediation. That the adversary might really wish the fighting to continue was a possibility too cruel to contemplate. Senator Mike Mansfield preferred to forget his words of 1964: "A reasoned approach to this situation on our part is no assurance that others will have the same capacity. Our own restraint is no guarantee of the restraint of others. Our wish for peace is not necessarily the wish of others."

When the first halt in bombing brought no peace, it seemed reasonable to suggest that the pause was not long enough. When the second suspension proved Hanoi still intractable, emphasis shifted to the desirability of yielding more — and more, and still more. Few Americans wished to recall the experience that lay behind the statement of Hanoi's deputy chief of staff to the Viet Cong congress of April 1966: "We will take advantage of the opportunity offered by the negotiations to step up further our military attacks. In fighting while negotiating, the side which fights more strongly will compel the adversary to accept its conditions."

Heated debates about the North Vietnamese state raged through the 1960s. Its defenders described it as a progressive country offering fraternal aid to southern nationalists. The events of the 1970s only confirmed what informed Americans knew years before: that a totalitarian, aggressive regime ruled the country from Hanoi and was willing to exterminate Trotskyites, nationalists, collaborationists, and any other challengers to its authority. Terror had given it power in 1945; terror remained its chosen instrument of government. The so-called boat people and other refugees, among them Truong Nhu Tang and Hoang Van Hoan of the Viet Cong, too late conceded that nationalism was but a front for Communism. North Vietnam violated all agreements when it dared and continued to do so during the long cease-fire negotiations; and the total American withdrawal left it free to pounce upon its neighbors once they were denuded of aid. North Vietnam meanwhile retained the support of both the Soviet Union and the People's Republic of China. Indeed, in the thinking of Lin Piao, the conflict in Vietnam was the cutting edge of a revolution that would ultimately spread around the world. Early lack of success may have been responsible for his mysterious disappearance; and the inability to arrive at a clear victory may also have widened the rift between the Soviet and the Chinese Communists.

President Johnson's critics long favored formation of a coalition government in South Vietnam, arguing that Saigon lacked popular support. French journalist Jean Lacouture expressed the view of many Frenchmen when he urged a truce that would admit the National Liberation Front (Viet Cong) to the government of South Vietnam. The premise of his prescription for peace was the proposition that the Viet Cong were truly independent of Hanoi and engaged in a genuine civil war. An independent South Vietnam, Lacouture acknowledged, was only the prelude to ultimate reunification on Ho's terms and the integration of Vietnam into an Indochinese union that would subject Cambodia and Laos to the same fate. Better the Communists than the American puppets! Lacouture wasted no tears over the economic failures north of the seventeenth parallel or the victims of Ho's purges. Americans like Arthur M. Schlesinger, Jr., who advocated in 1967 not United States withdrawal from Vietnam but a halt to bombing and a negotiated settlement, also looked fancifully to a coalition government. The effort to lure to the conference table those who wished to fight, not noticeably successful in the past, did not prove workable in the future.

Neither in 1967 nor at any time later was there evidence to quiet the fears expressed by Secretary of State Dean Rusk that yielding in Vietnam would only shift the scene of the fighting to some other area. Questioned about the domino theory in a television interview on September 9, 1963, President Kennedy replied passionately: "I believe it, I believe it." The fall of South Vietnam would "give the impression that the wave of the future in Southeast Asia was China and the Communists. So I believe it."

The will of the people was also foreseeable. The failure of the "Tet offensive" of 1968 demonstrated hostility to the Communists. Even where, as in Hue, the North Vietnamese held temporary control, they could not mobilize a following. Indeed, experience ultimately confirmed the worst fears of those who supported President Johnson's policy. A bloodbath did follow Saigon's collapse and spread across Laos and Cambodia. The dominoes did fall across the south of Asia. Visions of collective security and international law faded.

The Vietnam policy failed because the United States was unwilling to make the hard choices required of it in 1968. The Tet offensive that year was the turning point. The Communists knew what happened: there had been no popular support, despite the unrestrained use of force. Chairman Truong Chinh, lecturing party cadres in May of that year, acknowledged that the attack had been a catastrophe and called for protracted guerrilla warfare. But Americans did not know what happened. Former United States Ambassador to India John Kenneth Galbraith in February predicted "the disappearance of anything" that could effectively be called a government within "the next few weeks," while on United States campuses law school professors and their students protested against their country's policy. Shortly NBC announced, as if the result of a football game, that the United States had lost the war, an impression heightened by faulty press and television reporting.

The reluctance to follow through militarily after the repulse of the Red attack; the bombing halt; and the willingness to negotiate at length signaled weakness to Hanoi, which regrouped its forces and rearmed with weapons from the Soviet Union. Again in 1970, when the United States attack on Cambodian bases forced a Communist withdrawal, the pause at the conference table gave the North Vietnamese time to prepare for a new assault, while the gradual withdrawal of American troops and of aid left Saigon exposed when the Communists callously disregarded the terms of the truce and attacked, this time successfully and decisively.

The United States did not withdraw because of any mass revulsion in popular opinion. The majority of Americans continued to understand and to favor the prosecution of the war. Opinion did not shift until after bombing halts and peace talks made further struggle seem pointless. But an influential minority of dissenters, unwilling to acquiesce in the decisions of the majority, raised disconcerting problems at home, and also exposed the deeper issue of the role of dissent in a democracy.

Along with the damage in lives lost, bodies maimed, property destroyed, opportunity wasted, and diplomacy disoriented, the ultimate accounting of the costs of Vietnam will also have to consider its effects upon long-established understandings about the interrelationships among dissent, democracy, and foreign policy.

Restraints upon the right of citizens to disagree with the established course of government actions were less burdensome after 1960 than ever before in history. Dissenters spoke out vigorously against decisions approved by popular majorities through democratic procedures. The resultant tensions were severe, especially when they arose from disagreements over foreign policy, where the issues affected the security not only of the United States but also of the large part of the world that looked to it for leadership. Those tensions also affected the viability of democracy in the modern world.

The problem of reconciling dissent with diplomacy was peculiar to a free society, which could not emulate authoritarian regimes in suppressing discord. In the 1960s the stakes were grave and momentous. The elected leaders had the power to destroy the whole world; and their decisions involved considerations they could not always readily communicate to a wide public.

Dissenters had the right to speak out and make their views known. The majority had the right to set the limits within which decisions were made. Yet offsetting obligations qualified those rights at points of conflict. The majority could act but had to be cognizant of the privileges of dissenters. Dissenters could speak out but without impeding the right of the majority to decide. Leaders had to remain responsive to the views of both the majority and the minority. That delicate balance did not hold when it came to Vietnam.

Dissent is one of the cherished American rights. Together, the First and Fourteenth Amendments forbid Congress and the states to make any law abridging the freedom of speech, or of the press, or of the right of assembly. But recognition of the value of dissent antedated formal constitutional safeguards and had deep roots in social institutions and national character. Despite occasional infringements under the pressure of presumed or actual emergencies, the privilege of saying no without punishment was always an important ingredient of freedom in the United States.

The right to dissent was a useful device of the powerless who wished to assert views different from those of their rulers, but also possessed a moral character of its own. Since no human church could be truly certain of its own holiness or of its conformity with the divine precepts, it was best to allow each individual to follow his own conscience and to worship in his own way. Since there could be no certainty of the correctness of any propositions, no prince or potentate could impose his views on others. Nor, for that matter, could a scientist or expert use his knowledge to coerce others into accepting his opinions. Truth would triumph over error only through the open exposure of all points of view. "Who ever knew Truth put to the worse in a free and open encounter?" John Milton had asked. To give light was the task of the leader; the people could find their own way.

The liberal creed that safeguarded the right to dissent gained increasing acceptance in the nineteenth century. Freedom of expression was an essential element of human dignity, for it guaranteed respect for the conscience of every single being. Furthermore, by putting the progressive and the novel above authority and custom, dissent appealed to the American tendency to cherish the rugged individual and to value nonconformity. A common willingness to depart from accepted standards made heroes of critics and crusaders.

The problem was more difficult when dissenters took aim not at an absolute monarch or an authoritarian church but at the will of the majority. Not all nonconformists found places in the pantheon of American heroes. The Tories during the Revolution and the Copperheads during the Civil War claimed the right of dissent; and the dominant majority had to decide how far to accord the right to those who would not themselves respect it if they held power.

The principle served those who opposed not only the rule of the majority but also the procedures of law and order. The Ku Klux Klan of the Reconstruction period acted against racial equality, and the white citizens' councils of the 1950s dissented from the Supreme Court's doctrine of desegregation. Some college students occupied buildings to express their disagreement with the war in Vietnam, just as others attempted to exclude James Meredith, a black, from the University of Mississippi. A society that refused to define heresy could not define orthodoxy and had to concede the right to all. Dissenters objected not only to the dominant views of sexual morality and to restrictions on the use of drugs but also to the use of fluorine in the water supply and to the theory of evolution.

Democracy thus complicated the concept of dissent. Protest launched not against authority or tradition but against decisions by a popular majority ran counter to another fundamental principle: that government operated through the consent of the governed.

It did not follow from that principle that any given majority was always correct or just or capable of making the choices appropriate to any particular crisis. The deficiencies of democracy were well known. More than a century ago a conservative British statesman warned that popular governments were reluctant to face the truth, were prone to increase expenditures without providing the means, entered into wars from passion and not from reason, and were likely ignominiously to seek a peace that might endanger their independence. Moreover, the tyranny of a multitude could threaten liberty as much as the tyranny of a monarch.

Nevertheless, despite its shortcomings, majority rule furnished a moral basis for political action. The law enacted by consent was not simply a brutal use of force but an expression of the community's sense of order.

Open discussion in a free marketplace of ideas kept the government responsive to the will of the people and provided lawful means for effecting change. That freedom imposed on the dissenter the duty to obey when in disagreement, since the decision was not the act of a despot but of the citizenry. On the other hand, every participant in a democracy shared the responsibility for the measures taken in its name; and whoever believed some such measure wrong had to say so.

Consciousness of the shortcomings of majority rule placed procedural and substantive safeguards in the American system to prevent the abuse of minority rights. The majority could not act except through the processes of law; and some privileges, like those in the Bill of Rights, were altogether beyond its reach. John C. Calhoun, who early perceived the problem, proposed to give the minority of Southern slaveholders a veto over emancipation by the free-state majority. The underlying argument, occasionally repeated in other contexts, was that the intensity of commitment of the minority deserved special recognition as against the more diffuse commitment or apathy of the majority. But Americans rejected his solution at the time and after. They wished the will of the majority to prevail, although in ways that would infringe as little as possible upon the rights of the minority.

The tension between the rights of the majority and of the minority was least dangerous when the protest was verbal. The government that enjoyed popular support needed few limitations upon the freedom of speech. The arguments of the coffeehouse anarchists or the village atheist only sharpened the loyalty of the citizen and strengthened the faith of the churchgoer. The freedom to speak out was a useful corrective to complacency in a democracy.

The problem was altogether different when dissent took the form of refusal to act in accordance with the law or indeed of a determination to impede its execution. The minority under those circumstances might undermine the orderly procedures that were its own best safeguards.

The dissenter who went beyond speech to direct action appealed to conscience. A higher law than that of the state had to prevail. "In the forum of the conscience," Chief Justice Charles Evans Hughes explained, "duty to a moral power higher than the state has always been maintained." Men and women, outraged by the fugitive slave laws in the 1850s or by segregation in the 1950s, deliberately violated government-set rules out of a conviction that they could not obey measures so unjust.

The claim of conscience was easiest to recognize when set within a clear religious context. God spoke to those who heard his voice and commanded them not to heed the dictates of Caesar. Dissenters who appealed to conscience without a theistic basis had to demonstrate the authenticity of their convictions — prove that the refusal was not merely a matter of convenience or interest, or a stubborn insistence upon setting personal judgment against that of the majority, but an absolutely compelling imperative. Otherwise the desire of each person to follow his or her preference would "overturn all polities, and instead of government and order, leave nothing but anarchy and confusion." The government, Justice Robert H. Jackson pointed out, could not "let any group ride roughshod over others" simply because their consciences told them to do so. The National Advisory Commission on Civil Disorders pointed out in 1968 that defiance of the legal authorities by those convinced that they alone understood the truth created a climate "that tends toward the approval and encouragement of violence as a form of protest." It found that "a general erosion of respect for authority in American society and the reduced effectiveness of social standards and community restraints" reinforced the impulse to "go beyond constitutionally protected rights of petition and free assembly and resort to violence to attempt to compel alteration of laws and policies." And violence bred counterviolence

To differentiate themselves from the lawless, the conscientious dissenters who went beyond verbal protest had to give evidence of their integrity by accepting the consequences and acknowledging the right of the state to punish. This was the classical argument of Socrates, who rejected Crito's invitation to escape an unjust punishment and preferred to die "in innocence, a sufferer and not a doer of evil; a victim, not of the laws, but of men." Dissenters who claimed the right of conscience and then resorted to legal quibbling to evade the consequences weakened the moral basis of their position and put themselves on a plane with people who sought loopholes to evade tax obligations or those who drove through red lights when no policeman was watching.

The effectiveness of dissent depended not only on the justice of the cause and on the fervor of those who participated but also on the way in which they conducted themselves. The contrast between the orderly, decent behavior of the blacks who sat in at the lunch counters or boycotted Jim Crow buses and the mobs who jeered at them lent force to those protests. By contrast, the outrageous conduct of the people who objected to the court order to desegregate the Little Rock schools exposed the poverty of their dissent.

Total honesty and consistency was the only moral justification of those who took a stand against the majority. Since they claimed to be bound by conscience, they had to follow wherever the rule led without seeking special exemptions. Pacifists like the late A. J. Muste who muted their criticism of Hitler in order to justify American neutrality in 1941, or those Quakers who attacked the role of the United States in Vietnam but defended the violence of the Maoist Red Guards put themselves into an anomalous position. By the same token, when the blood poured over the records of a draft office turned out to be that of animals, it eroded the moral strength of the protestors who had asserted that it was their own.

The claim of conscience in a democracy could only exempt the individual from involvement. It could not justify the imposition of minority views on others. Thoreau refused to pay a poll tax that would support an unjust war and went to prison as a result; he did not try to prevent others from paying theirs. Roger Williams stated the whole issue concisely. Denying that he had ever argued for "an infinite liberty of conscience," he compared society to "a ship to sea, with many hundred souls" aboard, of whom some were Catholics and Protestants, others Jews and Turks. "All the liberty of conscience that ever I pleaded for turns upon these two hinges — that none of the Papists, Protestants, Jews or Turks be forced to come to the ship's prayers or worship" nor prevented from conducting their own if they wished. Notwithstanding this liberty, it was the duty of the captain to "command the ship's course, yea, and also command that justice, peace and sobriety be kept and practiced." If any seamen or passengers refused to "help, in person or purse, toward the common charges of defence; if any refused to obey the common laws and orders"; if any mutinied or "preached or . . . wrote that there ought to be no commanders or officers, . . . no laws nor orders, nor corrections nor punishments; . . . in such cases . . . the commander or commanders may judge . . . and punish such transgressors."

Three centuries after Williams wrote, the need for order aboard ship was greater than ever. The millions of interdependent individuals in a complex society could not all have their own way. They could sustain their common enterprises in freedom only within agreed-upon rules. The speed and graphic character of modern communications, with their bewildering succession of sensational images, were less conducive to reflection and calm debate than were the pamphlets and sermons that moved earlier Americans. Mercurial changes of mood could alter popular attitudes in a matter of months; and the fashions that swept through society could affect ideas as well as clothes. Under these conditions, rational discussion was essential and its conduct demanded both the freedom to dissent and the willingness to restrain dissent within the limits of law.

Democracy provided the mechanism. The question was: Would Americans have the patience to use it?

The role of dissent in a democracy was particularly complex when it involved foreign policy. Some of the most painful crises in American history arose from disagreements over the relations of the United States with other countries and led to excesses that seriously infringed upon minority rights. In the 1790s the Republic had to decide whether to remain neutral or to become involved in the great war between revolutionary France and the rest of Europe. Controversy led to passage of a sedition law that seriously impaired freedom of speech and to the Logan Act, which forbade private individuals from meddling in foreign affairs. So too, later, the conflicts with Mexico and Spain and the two world wars aroused bitter protest.

These issues trapped the presidents most swayed by liberal sentiments. When Thomas Jefferson felt that the very future of the Republic was at stake, he took arbitrary and extreme measures to defend the embargo. Abraham Lincoln suspended the writ of habeas corpus and censored the press. Woodrow Wilson seriously strained the Bill of Rights through enforcement of the espionage and sedition acts and through tight control of the news. Franklin Delano Roosevelt during

World War II condoned the incarceration of American citizens of Japanese descent in concentration camps and also measures to limit free speech. The willingness of these democratic leaders to abandon the general tolerance of dissent demonstrated the seriousness of the conflict with principle.

The unique element in foreign affairs was the state's obligation to defend itself. Internal disputes rarely threatened the very existence of government; conflict with another power might well do so. Since the people surrendered to it the right to use force directly, the state could not expose itself to assault from internal minorities or from foreign foes, but had to protect the common interest of all its members. In defending itself there might be points at which the demand for security called for a limitation of some liberties. The history of the past fifty years showed that espionage and subversion were real and not imaginary weapons; and every state had to guard against them. None could acquiesce in its own destruction.

Furthermore, the rules of conduct that ordinarily governed the behavior of the minority and the majority did not apply to the relationships among states, each a complex entity, composed of many groups and interests and yet presumed to act as if a unified whole. A conventional code of etiquette and law regulated the conduct of states with one another and sometimes impeded the exercise of the right to dissent.

Despite the aspirations of Woodrow Wilson for open covenants, openly arrived at, secrecy remained important in international affairs. No government could depart from the pattern so long as it dealt with others that insisted upon secrecy. Frequently indeed the peaceful outcome of negotiations depended upon understandings reached behind closed doors, away from the emotional pressures of popular opinion and the demands of prestige. The missile crisis of

1962 could not have been resolved with the efforts for détente conducted in the public view. Often, as in that case, the business before the diplomats involved third parties, and sometimes fourth, fifth, and sixth parties. In dealing with each other, the United States and the Soviet Union had to keep in mind the interests and wishes of allies as well as of opponents; and statesmanship consisted of maintaining a delicate balance among all the elements.

Secrecy inevitably complicated the relationship of the diplomat to the dissenter. Rarely was the full story known while talks were in progress, so that criticism was often ill informed. The critics who denounced the American government for failure to open negotiations on Vietnam in 1966 and 1967 did not know about the dozens of efforts to do so in those years. Since the public was less familiar with the nuances of diplomacy than with immediate domestic issues, dissenters rarely understood the complex problems statesmen faced. It was all too easy early in 1968 to call for vigorous action to obtain the return of the United States intelligence ship *Pueblo,* but the government had to keep in view the possibility that a nuclear confrontation might be the result of forceful action. To favor unilateral disarmament ignored the possibility that steps toward that end might actually bring war closer rather than postpone it.

The process of accommodation and compromise among competing groups, effective in domestic affairs, did not readily apply in international relations. In dealings with others, a state had to act as if a unifying common interest overrode internal divisions; and the need to speak with one voice altered the consequences of dissent.

In negotiations around the peace table, each state had to define and clarify its position, but also convince its antagonists that it was not bluffing. A miscalculation could have the most damaging consequences. In 1961, at their meeting in Vienna, Chairman Khrushchev delivered to President Kennedy what amounted to an ultimatum over Berlin. The president's response made it clear that the United States would fight rather than yield. Had substantial opposition at home weakened Kennedy's confidence, Khrushchev might have been tempted into an adventure with disastrous results for all.

The nation also had to maintain some continuity in its commitments to other states. Power rested not only on skillful diplomacy and the arms to back it up but also upon a network of understandings and mutually accepted obligations. A country that did not keep its promises, either because it chose not to or because internal divisions prevented it from doing so, lost both credibility and allies. Changes in foreign policy, appraised in terms of their effect upon the international order, therefore could not be abrupt or heedless of their consequences for others.

Some democracies consequently attempted to maintain bipartisanship in foreign policy, removing these issues entirely from domestic politics and entrusting them primarily to professional foreign-office experts. In Britain, Denmark, and the Netherlands, party changes in the government did not affect the underlying continuity of policy.

True bipartisanship was rare in the United States, however, other than in the few years after Pearl Harbor, when war united the country. Thereafter, as earlier, foreign policy was a recognized subject of political debate, although the important lines of division did not always coincide with those of party. There were isolationists and interventionists, hawks and doves, among both Democrats and Republicans.

Hence, American policymakers labored under an exceptional burden. On many day-to-day matters, and under the pressure of emergency even on major ones, they could not wait upon the results of a referendum, or rely upon polls, or even canvass all the interest groups involved, but had to act promptly. In doing so they also had to move within the ambit of general policies that they knew would command the support of the majority.

Much therefore depended upon the quality of public opinion; and dissenters, as much as the majority, bore the responsibility of educating rather than merely agitating the citizenry. Totalitarian regimes, not obliged to heed dissenters, thus had an advantage at the negotiating table. The Chinese, in the long, extended discussions at Panmunjom between 1951 and 1953, did not have to take account of disagreement at home, as the United States did. Nor in the Middle East crisis of 1967 did the Soviet Union have to worry about alienating blocs of voters during the Arab-Israeli war.

Critical bystanders had an enormous advantage over the diplomat who actually played the cards. The power of hindsight gave the dissenters the right to a second guess once the hand was down. More important, they did not have to count the stakes and could make promises without much concern about fulfillment. The critics of United States policy toward Vietnam benefited tremendously from the advantage of dissent. They could unreservedly urge negotiations to end the war or to form a coalition government in Vietnam. But diplomats knew that it took two to make peace, that wars ended not with announcement of a willingness to negotiate but only with an agreement on terms, and that while it was easy to pronounce abstractly in favor of coalition government, it was not easy to decide who would control the police and the army under such a regime. Experience after 1972, alas, confirmed the worst fears of the Johnson administration.

More generally, a democratic regime unwilling to drum up jingoistic emotions or suppress dissent was at a disadvantage as compared to its domestic critics. The burdens and responsibilities of office limited the opportunities for persuasion. A nonincumbent candidate could spend month after month on the hustings; the officeholder daily tackled the pile of business on his desk. The former could find fault and make proposals freely; the latter worried about consistency and weighed the meaning of every word. Senator Eugene McCarthy, for instance, on June 1, 1968, demanded both that the United States act through the United Nations and that it support Israel. The actual incompatibility of the two positions did not bother him. Yet, in the long run, it was more important to inform the citizens about difficult choices than to gain an electoral victory; dissenters who operated within the American system had a duty to contribute to the process of education.

The war in Vietnam evoked opposition from a variety of sources. Most critics of the United States government used the political process and the methods of discussion to express their disagreement. But some considered conventional protest inadequate and insisted on demonstrating their hostility through direct action.

Pacifists, through religious beliefs or conscientious conviction, abjured any use of violence. In the United States, the majority of citizens did not share that faith, which, in practice, refused to draw distinctions between the aggressor and the attacked. Yet although most Americans regarded it as their duty to obey the law even when it ran counter to their consciences, they conceded to Quakers and others the right to stand apart from actions considered wrong. But the logic of their position demanded that pacifists abstain from using violence, directly or indirectly, in espousing their positions. M. K. Ghandi explained, "We must refrain from crying 'shame, shame' to anybody, we must not use coercion to persuade other people to adopt our way. We must guarantee to them the same freedom we claim for ourselves." In other words, a morally grounded commitment to nonviolence in a democracy would not impede the operations of the state that allowed all to practice their own way. Nevertheless, many critics fastened upon isolated incidents at Son My or My Lai to cry "shame, shame," and to discredit the whole effort. And some, a decade later, hold their silence in the face of the abominable consequences of withdrawal.

Quite a different line of argument sustained the opposition of those who did not condemn war in general but maintained that the American course in Vietnam was unjust, illegal, or immoral. Such dissenters sometimes argued that President Johnson entered upon the conflict without proper authorization and by doing so embroiled the United States in a civil war, not properly its concern. They therefore considered it a duty not to cooperate with the government and to do whatever was needed to halt its criminal actions. The position was fallacious. A formal declaration of war was never required to allow the president, as commander in chief, to send American troops into battle. John Adams, who conducted a "quasiwar" with France; Woodrow Wilson, who dispatched forces into Mexico; Franklin D. Roosevelt, who authorized naval engagements with the Germans; and Dwight D. Eisenhower, who sent marines to Lebanon, were among the presidents who understood the utility of action short of a full-scale, unlimited war. The urgency of avoiding unlimited war, in a world armed with nuclear weapons, was greater than ever in the 1960s. In any case, Congress did authorize the actions taken after 1964 and would then have gone further if requested.

The military decisions after 1964, deliberately and legally made, were consistent with a foreign policy developed over two decades under the administrations of four presidents. That policy was defensive; in order to minimize the risk of nuclear war, it aimed to create conditions of international stability by resisting aggression, whether overt or under the cover of subversion. Wise or unwise, that policy was not, on the face of it, so immoral that it justified broadening dissent into direct action against the national institutions.

Finally, among the opponents of the war were a small minority of convinced enemies of the Republic, who rejected alike democracy, majority rule, and the methods of free discussion, and saw in Vietnam but one instance of the general corruption of American society. This heterogeneous band included orthodox Marxists, flaming Maoists and Castroites, and some anarchists. They talked not about conscience or rights, but about revolution; and they had in common only a burning sense of frustration and of alienation from their society. Glorifying Ho Chi Minh and the Khmer Rouge, they shared responsibility for the millions who subsequently lost their lives in Southeast Asia.

Some followers of Herbert Marcuse joined forces with these activists. Marcuse himself professed loyalty to true democracy and ultimately to a free society. But he insisted that the contemporary system of the United States was fraudulent and its freedom only apparent. The whole order, he argued, was so thoroughly integrated in defense of capitalism that even its superficial tolerance was only a means of subjecting the populace to the system. Therefore, its total destruction was necessary to liberate man.

Marcuse, a philosopher, did not supply the evidence to square his theories with reality. Any objective analysis of the developments of the decades after 1950 would show a steady enlargement of tolerance and of the scope of individual freedom in America. But his very vagueness permitted his disciples to disclaim any obligation for espousing a positive program until after they completed the destruction of the old order. At the same time his jibes at tolerance permitted his followers to insist that they alone knew the truth denied to others. That accounted for their hostility to majority judgments. Noam Chomsky expressed their mood when he argued that the failure of the peace march on Washington to alter the nation's foreign policy exhausted the available political alternatives, so it was time to shift from dissent to resistance. It did not occur to him that the failure to persuade the majority might be evidence of his own error.

The tolerance accorded these extremists was the best refutation of their criticism. Far from mechanizing their lives or flattening them out into one-dimensional men, this affluent society provided unparalleled latitude for a variety of styles of existence. It encouraged a greater range of freedom and was more involved in the quest for social justice than ever before in history. And it provided the machinery for alterations in policy through discussion and persuasion. Those who refused to use that freedom had only their shortcomings or inadequacies to blame.

The extremist fringe among the dissenters imposed a special responsibility upon those who did have faith in democracy and in the methods of rational discourse. People who opposed the war out of conscience or out of a concern for the preservation of American values should have disassociated themselves from those who wished to spread rather than curtail violence and to destroy rather than preserve freedom. Instead, all made common cause; and responsible citizens condoned methods that threatened the basis of both democracy and dissent — among them ridicule, contumely, and intolerance of opponents, unwillingness to listen to alternative points of view, disregard for legal procedures, and a leftist reign of terror on many college campuses. Many students learned to regard kindly Ho Chi Minh as the George Washington of his time. The American Association of University Professors refused to consider disruption of classrooms an abridgment of academic freedom; but a distinguished political scientist ponderously argued that defense of American foreign policy in 1967 "effectively limits free speech." Thereafter, Vietnam became the universal scapegoat on which to blame any failing.

Leonid I. Brezhnev knew better. Speaking in Moscow on November 3, 1967, he hailed the solidarity of the socialist countries helping the North Vietnamese and gloated over the declining international prestige of the United States.

When Abbie Hoffman and the Chicago Seven became cultural heroes in 1968, they not only assured the election of Richard Nixon but shook popular confidence in the judicial and political order incapable of restraining their rowdy antics. That year and in 1972 the peace candidates met overwhelming defeat at the polls. But the turbulence they created sapped the will to govern and prevented the reasonable consideration of any foreign policy, old or new.

By 1972 the dominant tone of the news media had turned hostile to American involvement in Vietnam, and the Nixon administration had embarked on the effort at extrication —

without, however, attempting to reconsider the whole line of policy that had led to the adventure in the first place. The gap in understanding persisted and deepened with time, for the passing years brought no reappraisal of America's role or the kind of world it wished to share with other peoples. Politicians and their critics, alike eager to evade the issues of the 1960s, simply assumed that those issues had gone away and shut their ears to reminders, in the toll of daily events, that aggression, subversion, and terrorism remained a legacy for the 1980s.

7

Loss of Will

THE PERCEPTIVE AND HONEST OUTSIDER NOTED a phenomenon Americans were themselves reluctant to perceive. He addressed a divided audience. Those who matched his observations against experience found them accurate in their diagnosis of disorder (though flawed in the understanding of the causes). Critics enclosed within ideological blinders indignantly rejected the validity of his message.

When Aleksandr Solzhenitsyn spoke at Harvard on June 8, 1978, he demanded and got attention. The speech was far longer than any heard at a Harvard commencement in the past century. Through that afternoon the rain fell steadily, and only the most foresighted among the listeners had brought umbrellas. Yet no one left. Occasionally the TV cameras swiveled and zoomed among the audience, capturing the rapt regard of people hearing an unwelcome message. The occasion moved those present not only for what Solzhenitsyn said, but also for what they found worthy of attention in his message.

Curiously, the reactions of most American intellectuals who commented on the address were unresponsive. Perhaps the failure of communication was due to distance: those not actually at the scene missed the impact of personality that reinforced the message. More likely, many who should have listened refused to hear what Solzhenitsyn had to say.

Read rather than listened to, Solzhenitsyn's address (published as *A World Split Apart*) proves diffuse, like much of Solzhenitsyn's writing since *Ivan Denisovich* — less an integrated, articulated argument than a series of successive piercing insights of prophetic quality. The theme was clear: loss of will in the West, reflected in a culture dominated by "the idols of the prevailing fad," in the disarray of social institutions, and in the inability to deal coherently with global problems. These failures sprang from the spirit of hedonistic individualism, the origins of which reached back to the Renaissance. Solzhenitsyn had sounded the same complaints before his arrival in America, for he spoke not only of the United States alone but of the West as a whole — and about that he knew something long before he left the Soviet Union.

His stance was familiar. Solzhenitsyn was one of a long line of Russian religious thinkers critical of the intrusion of Western influences that since the nineteenth century had threatened Slavic culture. But that Solzhenitsyn stood squarely in his own tradition and addressed Americans from that perspective did not make him any the less competent a critic. Indeed, distance permitted him to perceive in the West what proximity obscured for its residents, who should have read him as they did Dostoevski — to learn something of the difference in vantage point, and also to profit from the outsider's capacity to describe what the insider could not see.

Few news commentators understood what Solzhenitsyn had to say. Most treated the address as a media event. Some were simply abusive. "Hasty and superficial" was the judgment of columnist Ellen Goodman. "A fancy con job," wrote the *Boston Globe*'s Mike Barnicle, sneering at the Russian novelist for being driven around in a limousine and sounding like Joe McCarthy. To Olga Carlisle Solzhenitsyn was simply a nationalist. Mary McGrory, hurt and angered, had expected at least kind words from a guest of the nation who really desired a return to the good old czarist days. Edward C. Norton (*Nieman Reports,* Autumn 1978) slyly mentioned the "villas in Vermont that wealthy expatriate Russian writers can afford." Historians were no more perceptive: Daniel J. Boorstin labeled Solzhenitsyn's comments dyspeptic, while Barbara Tuchman wrote him off as a cult figure and William L. O'Neill as a reactionary speaking nonsense. Other comparisons were to General Curtis LeMay on Vietnam, to *Pravda* on American pornography, and to Spiro T. Agnew on the American press. True, most published letters to editors revealed a favorable reaction (like that of the audience in Harvard Yard); no doubt their writers lacked the intellectuals' sophistication.

Solzhenitsyn was not flattering in his comments on the press — on its psychic disease, hastiness, superficiality, and uniformity of fashion that shuts off independent thought. David Bromwich and other hostile critics interpreted these observations as a plea for censorship, thus supplying the evidence to support Solzhenitsyn's indictment of American journalism. The speaker in fact attacked not freedom of the press, but the use made of it, and pleaded not for government control but for inner responsibility, just as he called not for an end to legality but for a perception of its limitations. Nor did Solzhenitsyn desire a return to the past. In the peroration of his address he explained: "No one on earth has any other way left but — upward," for a major watershed in history demanded a rise to a new height of vision, a new level of life, "where our physical nature will not be cursed, as in the Middle Ages, but even more importantly, our spiritual being will not be trampled upon, as in the Modern Era." No more damning charge could be brought against the journalists and others who tilted with him than their inability to read or report him accurately.

Solzhenitsyn touched a raw nerve by referring to Vietnam. In response, Robert Coles proffered opposition to the war as proof of the durability of American freedom; and the *Boston Globe* lauded the moral courage of the protestors. For on this delicate subject, in 1978, the American consensus was: forget. Former hawks and former doves alike agreed that there was no profit in recalling that disagreeable subject. Solzhenitsyn insisted on reminding them all that the consequences of Vietnam had not and would not go away. That was the speaker's unforgivable transgression.

The realpolitiker, of course, had never had a problem. All along, George Kennan, Hans Morgenthau, and Stanley Hoffman had linked policy to cost/benefits; and they assessed the results as they would the score of a game. To them Solzhenitsyn had nothing to say, other than to report the roars of laughter in Moscow's Old Square at the pronouncements of these political wizards.

But the intense concern with Southeast Asia that suffused the years after 1967 also sprang from moral judgments about the character of the conflict; and in effect Solzhenitsyn demanded a review of those judgments now.

Mention of Vietnam recalled the faded expectations of 1968, when Eugene McCarthy and Robert Kennedy had insisted that only a little give would persuade the Viet Cong to enter a coalition government in which Communists would not necessarily be the majority. Other opponents of the war demanded respect for the will of the people — those doughty little fighters on bicycles. Still others, in pacifist purity, insisted that unilateral withdrawal would lead to peace. A decade had passed. As to the prospect for a non-Communist coalition, nothing was said because there was nothing to say. The illusion was never more than the wishful thinking of Americans who had learned nothing from the experience of Eastern Europe. But as to the will of the people, there was much to say that was not being said. The word came almost at once from Cambodia, from Laos, and from Vietnam — and it continued to come by way of the refugee camps — of the desperate plight of the boat people and of a war that American withdrawal did not end. Its letters spelled enslavement.

The question might well have been asked: What was there to discuss? The answer was moral responsibility.

"Members of the U.S. antiwar movement became accomplices in the betrayal of Far Eastern nations," said Solzhenitsyn, "in the genocide and the suffering today imposed on thirty million people there." The convinced pacifists did not hear the moans coming from there. Nor did they understand their responsibility. They preferred not to hear. Thus, Solzhenitsyn. Lyndon Johnson agonized over each day's bombing targets. Who mourned the victims of 1978?

The United States no more confronted the choice of war or peace in 1968 than it did in 1941. Nor a choice of coalition or anti-Communist governments. Nor even a choice of bombing or not bombing targets that would save lives and spare the dikes. The actual choice — the only choice — was between war, with all its horrible risks and consequences, and surrender to totalitarian aggressors whose appetite grew with the feeding. The clatter heard out of Angola, Ethiopia,

Afghanistan, and Iran was the sound of falling dominoes, as awareness of Western paralysis eased restraints upon assaults from within and without.

The *New York Times* editorialists (June 13, 1978) considered Solzhenitsyn's attitude toward Communism an obsession. Perhaps. Almost exactly 120 years before, an American responded to the same charge — obsession — when it was leveled against citizens concerned with slavery in far-off states. In June 1858 Abraham Lincoln, quoting the New Testament, noted that "a house divided against itself cannot stand." The Union could not endure permanently half slave and half free. He did not expect the Union to be dissolved, but he did expect that it would cease to be divided. It would become all of one thing or all of the other. Drawing from the same source as Lincoln, Solzhenitsyn warned of the danger of disaster from manifold splits, deeper than they appeared at first glance, "in accordance with the ancient truth that a kingdom — in this case, our Earth — divided against itself cannot stand." This was a warning Americans habituated to thinking of one world should have heeded.

The moral issue in 1978 as in 1858 was that of neutrality. Not all bystanders are consigned to the hottest fires in hell Dante set apart for them; though the bell tolls for all, those powerless to intercede may be forgiven for turning their backs. Not so those who waste the strength that might make a difference.

Solzhenitsyn probably did not know the detailed pathology of the Kitty Genovese syndrome, which shocked and surprised Americans at its dramatic first manifestation in the public murder of a nurse in Queens, New York, while onlookers ignored her pleas for help. But he recognized later symptoms: the decline of civic courage in the West, "particularly noticeable among the ruling and intellectual elites," which led to depression, passivity, and perplexity, and even more so to "self-serving rationales as to how realistic, reasonable, and intellectually and even morally justified it is to base state policies on weakness and cowardice."

The concern with personal well-being and the erosion of the capacity for voluntary self-restraint contributed to those enervating tendencies. Legalistic relationships created an atmosphere of spiritual mediocrity "that paralyzed man's noblest impulses" and tilted freedom toward evil. Solzhenitsyn here undervalued the protection Western law offered the individual against the state. But he discerned the bizarre legalisms by which the guilty escaped conviction, the protracted procedural delays that in themselves were a denial of justice, and the developing labyrinth of privilege that created inequality in the eyes of the law. (Not even the novelist could have conceived the twist of fortune that allowed terrorist Weathermen to go free and convicted the FBI agents who defended the country against them.)

The media abused their tremendous power. Commercially motivated, given to sensationalism, hasty and superficial in judgments, the electronic and print media alike stoked hedonistic, isolationist impulses. Scholarly studies have revealed in intimate detail the way in which newspapers and television distorted information on Vietnam and on the election of 1968. The same patterns persisted in 1978 in identification of the African Marxists as the "patriotic front" and of the Lebanese Christians as "right-wing" and in 1979 in reporting or not reporting events in China and Iran. Crisis-oriented, episodic, sensational reporting thus kept from Americans any hint of the ethnic diversity of the Iranian population while it might have been useful, just as the same attitudes blocked out information on popular resistance to Mao's regime.

Solzhenitsyn clearly disclaimed any intention of making a comprehensive survey of the civilization that gave him shelter. He only "mentioned a few traits of Western life which surprise and shock a new arrival to this world." Much about the West, and particularly about the United States, remained a closed book to him. He knew little of the humanitarianism that impelled the effort to elevate popular life from the brutal struggle for survival to a spiritual plane where justice infused politics and fear of hunger ceased to shape the economy. Nor was Solzhenitsyn conscious of the universalism that persuaded Westerners of the unity of the lot of mankind; nor of the striving for improvement, sparked by the conviction that a divine element flickered in the least of human beings.

Nineteenth-century Russian novelists sometimes mocked the Westernizer's glib prattling about progress; but they knew the ideas they mocked. Solzhenitsyn did not.

How could he? Where would a visitor to the United States in the 1970s learn about these neglected features of the American, the Western, past. Archie and Edith, Laverne and Shirley, Mork and Mindy, Starsky and Hutch — jeering, japing caricatures crammed the screens, big and little, so that only the *Star Wars* robots and the Muppets enlisted the human sympathy of the viewer. There was much more to the United States and to the West than the media displayed; but a foreigner could not discover the positive features in the dominant forms of cultural expression. Archibald MacLeish, regretfully noting that Solzhenitsyn had not done his homework, advised the Russian to get out and meet his fellow writers. However, were Aleksandr Isayevich to arrive at a literary cocktail party, he would have had to avoid the Vidals, the Coovers, the Doctorows, who owed places on the best-seller lists to systematic falsification and denigration of their country. And among serious writers of fiction, drama, and poetry, he would have been hard put to find a single one whose work failed to emphasize the spiritual malaise, personal and social, of which Solzhenitsyn spoke.

Nor would he have discovered the meaning of progress from Pete Seeger, green grass rising through the concrete; or from historians like Theodore Roszak, who urged Americans to learn from "American Indian lore, Zen, and Tantra," or from L. S. Stavrianos, who wished to emulate Khmer Rouge austerities. Few historians of the United States in the 1970s said a kind word of their country's past and traditions.

It was hardly surprising, though regrettable, that a stranger, arriving from a totally different tradition found the spiritual aspects of the life about him obscure; they were hardly known to those who had long inhabited the country. Nor was it surprising that those unwilling to assess his honest criticism squirmed away from their own responsibility for occasioning it.

The conditions that evoked Solzhenitsyn's criticisms also evoked the unwillingness to heed his message. The affluent individuals of a society unaware of common goals and purposes turned inward; they narrowed interests to immediate gratification and tuned out appeals to any wider concerns.

In the thirty years after 1950, the dominant tone of American ideas shifted. The intellectuals who lived through World War II and the Depression formulated the social agenda commonly regarded as liberal or progressive. Heirs of John

Dewey and Oliver Wendell Holmes and Louis D. Brandeis, many had immigrant, farming, and wage-earning origins. They were alive to the uses of power and conscious of the realities of life on the margin of existence. After 1950, affluence and the increase of white-collar occupations magnified the importance of writers, readers, and viewers who led sheltered existences in professional and paraprofessional careers, set off in suburbs or in urban enclaves. Reality then receded and transformed the most influential liberal attitudes from a hard, often painful, array of commitments into a soft, comforting bundle of sentiments.

Three changes, among others, illustrated the distortion of the standard liberal agenda:

From freedom to permissiveness. Early in the twentieth century, progressive proposals included measures to free individuals and groups from irrational restraints inherited from the past and serving the interests or prejudices of the privileged. Discrimination, censorship, and inequality of opportunity were among the visible targets, against which broad sectors of the politically active mobilized. But the liberals of John Dewey's generation never believed that success in those efforts would lead to the disappearance of all restraints and responsibilities. Perhaps naively, perhaps with undue optimism, they expected the elimination of the old to make room for new, voluntarily generated, rational, progressive relationships between the individual and the community, with standards of behavior even stricter than in the past because attuned to present needs. Repeal of Prohibition would reduce drunkenness; free speech would promote sober discussion and high literary art while discouraging pornography; enlightened divorce laws would strengthen the family; and equal opportunity would bring merit to the fore. The distinction between ends and means was clear in anticipation.

The actual development was different. All those careful distinctions vanished with the tidal flow of material objects that swept across the American landscape after 1950. The abandonment of old restraints too often meant the abandonment of all restraints. In a culture increasingly devoted to sensation, gratification of immediate wants became the supreme, often the sole, criterion of good; and individuals devoted to mindless egocentric hedonism spared little thought for what they owed their neighbors. Little-used faculties shrank from the intellectual effort needed to distinguish between the freedom to publish *Ulysses* and the freedom to exhibit *Deep Throat,* between divorce as a recourse against intolerable abuse and the "split kit" that permitted separation at whim. And in the end self-indulgence only deepened the frustration of some and drove others to cultist obscurantism.

The degree to which Americans yielded to the new trends varied with occupation, income level, and place of residence. The educated, the professional, the well-to-do, and the urban were most susceptible and were thus identified in the most popular cultural media — novels, television, and movies. Family structure and religious identity — the historic defenses against analogous tendencies in the past — did not protect such mobile, rootless people. Neither "puritanism," the traditional hostility to epicureanism, nor the Enlightenment's insistence upon the purposeful character and the connectedness of human experience saved Americans from surrender to the temptation of immediate sensation. Freedom ceased to be deliberate rational choice, became indiscriminate yielding to impulse.

By 1980 the countertrend among bewildered blue-collar

workers, rural families, and the middle classes of the small towns encompassed those who claimed to represent the nation's moral majority. But the movement lacked effective intellectual spokesmen, could not define a coherent position on important issues, and expended its energies in symbolic protest. Its chief effect was to arouse suspicion and distrust of the media, the bureaucracy, Congress, the courts, and academia — indeed, of all established institutions — a result few really wished. It did not halt the slide to permissiveness.

From moral decision to utopianism. Anyone can vote for the angels against the devils. Such is not usually the choice presented. Much more real and much more difficult is the need to decide between more-than-less good and less-than-more evil. The colonists of 1770, loyal to the Crown, five years later knew that they had to fight for independence. The abolitionists, pacifists in the 1850s, knew in 1861 that only victory in battle would eradicate Southern slavery. Brandeis and Dewey were against war, but in 1917 supported Wilson against the kaiser.

Somewhere liberals lost the ability to make such choices. Turning away from the fantasy world of movie or television screen, they were blinded by the glare of reality. The gallery of their overseas villains since 1950 reached from Syngman Rhee to the shah of shahs. But were those really worse than the genuine, the only, alternatives — from Kim Il Sung to the Ayatollah Khomeini? Few Americans in 1980 would have answered in the affirmative — not once they learned of the secret trials and summary executions of physicians and teachers, of homosexuals and prostitutes in Iran. In 1980 "gangland warfare, waged by godfathers dressed in guerilla olive or clerical black" shocked the *New York Times* (July 28); it might have been aware of the danger at least a year earlier. Yet many liberals hastened to damn Rhee and the shah — along with Chiang, Diem, and others — by an abstract standard of excellence, indeed of saintliness.

The passionate condemnation lavished on the rogues was utopian. No consideration of the best available, of as good as possible under the circumstances, could stand against an abstract standard. To affirm the absolute virtue of a peace-loving, humane, liberal democracy in Iran in 1978 or in Korea in 1951 was beside the point and obscured the actual choice — between Kim and Rhee, between the shah and the ayatollah.

The utopian haze shrouded illusory dreams of wish fulfillment. If only the Sunni and Shiite would love one another, or the Greeks and Turks, or the Ulsterites and the Irish Republican Army, or the Basques and the Spaniards, or the Pakistani and Bengali, then violence would cease. A Latin America free from Central Intelligence Agency interference and from economic involvement with the United States would flower in stability. A Palestinian state on the West Bank would bring peace to the Middle East. Decolonization and the removal of white settlers (except the productive ones) would allow the less developed countries to flourish. But if not? And meanwhile? Where would the refugees in Lebanese camps go? And what if an Idi Amin made life intolerable for whites? There were no intermediate answers. The general blur clouded the issues.

Among the unreal choices that fluttered through the 1960s and 1970s, none was sadder than that of unilateral disarmament — as if the only risk were that of being better Red than dead. If worse came to worst, the argument ran, the USSR would take over and the West might well have to endure several decades of Soviet dictatorship. In the long run, moral and technical superiority would win out. But the probable outcome would be Red *and* dead; for no Communist state has displayed the capacity to rule without terror, to accommodate internal differences, or to preserve itself against fragmentation. Nuclear disaster would be far more probable than now in a world dominated by atom-bomb-brandishing commissars persuaded of their correctness by religious zeal.

From universalism to particularism. No change was as curious and as abrupt. Even in the relatively isolationist 1930s, liberals believed in the unity of the human kind, in the interdependence of people everywhere, and in the convergence of various social and political forms and values. By the 1940s the rhetoric of one world was commonplace. Basic to this faith was the understanding that men and women everywhere were so alike that common norms, values, and expectations applied to all.

Many liberals realized that cultural circumstances produced differences in practice. The swaddled Russian babies, anthropologists explained, were predisposed to authoritarianism; the German father image, psychologists pointed out, produced an obsession with order. Never mind. In time, convergence would bring them all together.

The evidence of the 1950s and 1960s was encouraging. Despite the impedimenta of its culture, Japan evolved into a Western democracy. Russian babies, swaddled or not, grew up contributors to *samizdat* published clandestinely by dissidents; and liberal values survived under adverse circumstances in East Germany, Poland, Hungary, and Czechoslovakia. And in the 1970s, despite the warnings of the experts about the weight of Confucianism, those same liberal values were splashed across the wall posters at the first lifting of Maoist repression. Faith in universalism ought to have been stronger in 1980 than ever before.

Not so fast! In fact, the application of identical standards and expectations around the world required a fortitude liberalism had lost. Neutralism bred habits of apology for regimes people did not wish to resist. Castro promised an election within six months; but Cubans had no interest in formal democracy. Nor did Angolans, or Ethiopians — or, for that matter, almost any of the liberated colonies. Nor were they interested in personal or intellectual freedom. The norms of laws and behavior valid for the United States and its allies somehow did not apply to people elsewhere; employing a common standard would have called for disturbing judgments and actions. It was easier to deplore the lack of civil liberties in South, but not North, Korea; in South, but not North, Vietnam. Never mind the fate of Asians in Kenya or of the victims of agrarian reform in Tanzania. It was only appropriate to hand over the fugitive Russians, North Koreans, and Cambodians to their countries. The American Political Science Association canceled a meeting in Chicago when the Illinois legislature failed to ratify the Equal Rights Amendment; APSA members participated in a meeting in Moscow devoted to peace, development, and knowledge. The Joint Committee on Latin American Studies, after a visit as guests of Cuba's Ministry of Foreign Relations in 1976, reported that the nature of that country's social science was due more to "youth and inexperience" than to "the repression of intellectual freedom." Pictures of the boat people or of starving Cambodians evoked pity; but liberals sedulously refrained from reflecting about the regimes that produced those results. The implications were too uncomfortable to contemplate. If those wretched victims were of the same clay as we, did they not deserve what we desire — bread but also liberty?

Pictures pass across the screen — of death and desolation in Sahel and Ogaden, of flaming buildings in Beirut and Baghdad, of camps on the Thai borders. At least the victims are not ours. We no longer ask for whom the bell tolls. Since it is not for us (or me), we do not care.

Neutralism becomes an entrenched habit of mind in a society of egocentric individuals. Those who bar their doors against events in the street, whether from fear, prejudice, or hopelessness, lose the capacity to act. They stay out of it, more often fail to vote than not, and put the interests of neighborhood over town, town over state, and state over nation — all because they see the world revolve about the pinpoint of their own identity. And American intellectuals, subject to the same cultural forces as others in their society, remain largely oblivious of changes to which they should have been most sensitive.

When Solzhenitsyn decried the loss of will in the West, he described this attitude. Neutralism is another term for the psychological weakness he detected. The search for easy ways out, the evasion of problems, and the effort to gain time by concession, amounted, the Russian observer believed, to betrayal.

8

Democracy and the Intellectuals

EUGENE MCCARTHY, George McGovern, and John Anderson had more in common than the disregard for conventional party politics in their bids for the presidency. Their independent stance attracted followers of much the same background and interest; and the candidates offered the electorate much the same qualifications. Not one of these contenders had had executive experience by which voters could judge their fitness. All three had served in the national legislature, but no one of them could claim credit for a substantial piece of legislation.

They nevertheless evoked passionate support. They did so by stating positions as debaters do, arousing substantial enthusiasm, though not enough for election. Their adherents believed them correct on important issues and judged correctness more important than other qualifications for the presidency. That judgment said much about the three men, about the nature of their appeal, and about their supporters.

McCarthy, McGovern, and Anderson were academics — not so much in the sense that two of them had actually begun their career as college teachers, but in the sense that all of them considered possession of the correct answers a sufficient claim to power. They were not the first such comets to appear in the American political skies. But they gleamed with exceptional brightness because of the vast increase in the number of voters ready to honor that claim as the result of a general yearning for answers.

The subsidence of fighting in Korea and the subsequent prosperity unsettled many Americans and raised questions about national goals — questions that few had asked during the war, when victory had been sufficient purpose. The disheartened had read Arnold Toynbee before 1939, Oswald Spengler even earlier, and Brooks Adams and Henry Adams long before. After 1960 the optimists joined pessimists in collective introspection. That year *Life* magazine devoted issue after issue to the subject of national purpose, which remained a perennial topic for speculation.

Late in life, Walter Lippmann, the ablest and most influential of twentieth-century American political thinkers, revealed the sources of that pervasive concern. Lippmann put into words the attitudes of a group that would grow more numerous and more important in the quarter-century after he wrote and that would carry the same ideas in a direction he could not anticipate. More than any of his contemporaries, he had gained the position to which all intellectuals aspired: he was listened to and he mattered. Scarcely out of college in 1910, he had found a respected place in journalism and for more than five decades set his opinions before attentive policymakers.

Lippmann's *Essays in the Public Philosophy* (1955) voiced fear about a historic catastrophe about to overtake Western society. He had felt the premonition in 1938 at the approach of another world war with the democracies unprepared and unarmed; and events had justified his foreboding. His analysis explained the cause of the disaster. Under the terrible pressure of World War I, the statesmen of the democracies lost courage, feared to demand the necessary sacrifices of their people, and shifted the responsibility for decisions to the masses. There could be no lasting peace after 1918, there could be no adequate preparation for the inevitable war in the 1930s, and there could be no orderly settlement of the issues raised by the defeat of fascism after 1945. The masses, lusting after soft solutions and incapable of assimilating complicated information, obstructed the measures necessary to their own salvation; and the helpless democracies drifted to their doom. Only restoration of the appropriate positions of governed and governors could halt the decline.

The factual flaws in the argument are less important than the underlying interpretation that Lippmann had long expounded. Distrust of the popular element in American government and uneasiness about the direction of democratic development were recurrent themes in his writing and thinking. In *A Preface to Politics,* in *Drift and Mastery,* in *The Phantom Public,* and in other books, he worked toward a broad theory of politics fully expressed in *The Public Philosophy.*

In Lippmann's longer view, the significant break came not in 1917 but in 1789. For two thousand years belief in a law above the ruler and the people, above the whole community of mortals, had dominated the practice of government. Toward the end of the eighteenth century, however, the "Jacobins," resentful of their exclusion from the government, destroyed public faith in that law and used the conception of popular sovereignty to justify their own seizure of power. Pulling down rather than conserving authority, preoccupied with power, they arrived finally at the doctrine that their ends justified any means. As Jacobinism gained currency, it stifled the traditions of civility, of liberty, equality, and fraternity, and of the Public Philosophy rooted in respect for natural law. "The enfranchised masses have not, surprisingly enough, been those who have most staunchly defended the institutions of freedom," Lippmann asserted.

Lippmann in 1955 urged all men to accept the supremacy of natural law. The Public Philosophy, he conceded, had been elastic enough to embrace the despots of the past — the Roman imperial order, medieval feudalism, the absolutism of the seventeenth century. But it could guard against those of the future if everyone now recognized it, if governors ruled in accordance with principles "upon which all rational men of good will, when fully informed," tended to agree, if the governed acquiesced in the decisions of the governors.

The unwillingness to understand what natural law meant to those who expounded it accounted for Lippmann's accusation that the Jacobins were responsible for its decline. Historically, Europeans associated the concepts of liberty, equality, and fraternity with the French Revolution. The Declaration of the Rights of Man and the Citizen gave natural law its widest currency in the nineteenth century; and the thinkers among whom there was continuity of ideas, from Diderot and Voltaire to Jefferson and Condorcet, were its great defenders. They, above any others, insisted upon constitutional process and the rule of law; and they most consistently upheld the traditions of civility, of liberty, equality, and fraternity.

It was no coincidence, therefore, that the firmest barriers against the encroachment of twentieth-century totalitarianism appeared in the United States, in Great Britain, in France, and in Scandinavia, where liberal democratic traditions were strongest. The polities least capable of resistance were those in which the established order stifled liberal democracy. Comparison of the states that survived with those that fell — the United States or France with Russia or Germany — revealed the error in Lippmann's assertion and in the line of argument it followed.

Lippmann's indictment of what Americans understood as democracy revealed a deep animus against the "masses" — that is, against the people whose uninformed whims, prejudices, and passions expressed in public opinion prevented statesmen from following a rational course. That animus, which had roots in the context of ideas that shaped his development as a publicist, remained part of the heritage he left his readers.

Lippmann was not a conservative. He proclaimed himself still a liberal democrat, and although he had turned his face against many ideas associated with liberalism and democracy, he had a valid claim to that affiliation. With regard to society, his expectations were those of the Progressives of the first decade of the century. The reformers of the time were by no means a homogeneous group. But some of the intellectuals among them — Herbert Croly, Lincoln Steffens, and the writers for the early *New Republic* — defined a political position that supplied Lippmann's ultimate point of reference and that explained why he believed in the 1950s that democracy, not totalitarianism, was on the decline. The Western governments, he asserted, needed the "strong medicine" that dictatorships supplied and that Hitler understood with "the insight of genius" — the longing of the masses to be ruled. The totalitarian state, Lippmann believed, was more capable of governing. An aura of majesty surrounded its rulers and evoked obedience. That aura emanated from the popular belief that the elite had subjected itself to a code and a discipline and had dedicated itself to ends that transcended personal desires.

This judgment was delusive. Few Nazi or Bolshevik bosses

were ever naive enough to ride through town protected by their aura of majesty alone. The very existence of elaborate regimes of terror showed their unwillingness to rely only on loyalty for obedience. The enormous power the totalitarian state disposed was usually sufficient to stifle resistance. But when the occasion presented itself, the masses demonstrated an inclination to desert, which revealed that they did not altogether love their rulers.

Furthermore, the same yardstick by which Lippmann measured the decline of the democracies also revealed the weakness of the dictatorships. Nothing in the Western record equaled in ineptitude the comic quadrille in which Hitler, Stalin, Yosuke Matsuoka, and Mussolini played at being partners between 1939 and 1941 — and without the distractions of public opinion. No American error after the war matched in magnitude the Soviet blunders that helped create the Marshall Plan and NATO and restored the power of Western Europe. The as-yet-unknown causes of Khrushchev's Cuban adventure, of the split with China, of the expulsion from Anwar Sadat's Egypt, or of the change of Afghan regimes revealed not shrewd Soviet calculation but floundering blindness fully as dangerous.

Lippmann's appraisal of the superiority of the totalitarian powers proceeded not from the evidence but from his (and the Progressives') definition of political leadership. The "natural and necessary duties" of a government, he wrote, "have to do with the defense and advancement abroad of the vital interests of the state and with its order, security, and solvency at home." The people who happened to be residents of the state knew only their own personal interests, not those of the community; as voters, therefore, they could not formulate policy. The true public interest — "what men would choose if they saw clearly, thought rationally, acted disinterestedly and benevolently" — should be arrived at much the way a series of equations was solved; and assemblies elected by the masses were incapable of solving equations. Informed leaders were.

This was the inner core of Lippmann's Progressivism. The disinterested social engineer was most at home in the higher mathematics of politics. Back then, in the youth of the century, the intellectuals nurtured the dream of a total reform of their society. Human nature was malleable, and they, the elite, would reshape the suffering masses. Their ideas would unfold in plans of action implemented through politics.

The plans were not realized; the outcome was not what the necessities of logic dictated. The Senate grew no wiser through direct elections; the graduated income tax did not produce equality; civil service reform protected an entrenched and steadily growing bureaucracy; the recasting of municipal charters did not eliminate the difficulties of the cities; and disarmament weakened defenses while encouraging belligerence. Yet the intellectuals and others who had put their faith in the idea, the expert, and the plan knew that they had seen clearly, thought rationally, and acted disinterestedly and benevolently. The fault had not been in themselves but in the brute masses, incapable of receiving the idea, unable to follow where led. In 1955 Walter Lippmann had come a long way intellectually since the days when he went to work for Lincoln Steffens. But in the face of the intractable democratic populace, he felt the same discomfort as did the Progressives of his youth. And no more than they did he understand wherein the popular conception of government differed from his own. Nor did his intellectual heirs in 1980.

The people did not hold that the end of government was to advance the interests of the state, but rather that it was to "establish justice, insure domestic tranquility, provide for the common defense, promote the general welfare, and secure the blessings of liberty." Politics was thus one of a variety of means of social action directed at important goals. The people considered themselves competent to judge the degree to which particular acts approached or fell short of their general social ends. Political decisions did not consist in the discovery of mathematically correct solutions to equations but rather in choices among feasible alternatives that might advance the interests of the greatest number.

Hence the people did not often turn for guidance to an intellectual elite. "Providence," they believed, "never intended to make the management of public affairs a mystery, to be comprehended only by a few persons of sublime genius." Rather, like the Lilliputians, they supposed that "truth, justice, temperance, and the like" were "in every man's power, the practice of which virtues, assisted by experience and a good intention, would qualify any man for the service of his country"; and generally in "choosing persons for all employments" they had "more regard to good morals than to great abilities."

They were not wrong. "Successful democratic politicians," Lippmann wrote, "are insecure and intimidated men." The roster of the most successful American politicians disproves the assertion — Washington, Jefferson, Jackson, Lincoln, the Roosevelts, Wilson, and Truman. None among them were the insecure and the intimidated. And although some of them stirred up controversy and some of them aroused the bitter antagonism of their opponents, none of them failed either to gain a full measure of trust from the majority of the people and all the powers needed to govern as an executive within the Constitution.

In the quarter-century after 1955, the intellectuals' distrust of liberal democracy deepened. Scientists and other academics entered the upper levels of the government bureaucracy in ever greater numbers, and the scope of federal actions steadily broadened. Ever more decisions about ever more matters took form in planning papers that imposed upon the people choices they did not make but that were good for them. Of course, disagreements over policy divided the brightest and best; and leaks to the media became the common mode of appeal from decisions of line superiors. Those who prevailed and those who did not ended up alike aggrieved.

The losers in the debates could at least take satisfaction in the shortcomings of actuality, convinced that the outcome would have been better had the government followed an alternative course. But the winners had no such consolation. Too often the formulas proved inadequate or inappropriate; the economy did not respond as it should have, or the educational system, or racial order, any more than did international relations. Only those who criticized without responsibility for action could be sure of satisfaction. And men and women whose capital was knowledge and whose stock in trade was correctness could not readily admit to having been wrong. Again and again, the blame fell upon the intractable people, upon the politicians they elected, and upon the government made cumbersome by the need to accommodate so many wills.

A like-minded audience agreed — an audience composed of other people whose capital was knowledge and whose interests were congruent to those of the intellectuals. The professional and paraprofessional occupations now numbered millions of practitioners — college graduates, suburbanites, often beneficiaries of the affluence two-income families made possible. Habituated to reading reviews if not books and therefore susceptible to the whims of fashion, they considered themselves disinterested, presumed to speak for the society at large, and took an attitude of condescending benevolence toward the blue-collared, hard-hatted masses. The same audience provided McCarthy, McGovern, and Anderson a following; and repeated disappointment at the polls deepened disillusionment with popular democracy.

The low esteem of liberal democracy and anti-Americanism fed upon one another. For generations, the New World had existed to right the evils of the Old; and it remained so for the world's masses. Wherever people could express themselves freely, polls regularly showed the United States to be the most admired foreign nation. Everywhere, ordinary men and women given a chance to vote with their feet made the same choice; in the 1960s and 1970s it remained the preferred destination among all people in flight. And where the least gleam of freedom flickered, popular culture revealed American influence, in Moscow as in Paris. Anti-Americanism, the sentiment of an intellectual elite, was more widely diffused where powerful political organizations, whose interests it served, gave it currency.

Hostility to the United States sprang in part from the intractability of its political system, in part from its materialism — that is, from its pervasive vulgarization of life. From Henry Adams to Ezra Pound to Norman Mailer, the certainty of knowing better than others corrupted artists and writers who aspired directly or indirectly to govern and who came to hate the people who refused to follow, yet came to admire the man of power who used them. At the same time, intellectuals judged their country harshly because they regarded it as the prototype of a culture built upon possession, upon the diffusion of an idolatry for material things — an idolatry associated with the common man. The ever-present fear of the intellectual was of being swamped by the masses, who threatened to crush cherished cultural values in the heedless pursuit of their own interests. The popular will endangered not only politics, where it insisted upon wrong preferences, but every aspect of life. The comfortable audiences that snickered at *MacBird* set themselves apart from the likes of the Johnsons and Kennedys.

Personal preferences, from this perspective, endangered the economy because American — that is, capitalist — society controlled people's options through advertising and the appearance of free choice. Their own false consciousness prevented the masses from realizing that what they thought they wished really differed from what they would have wished had they really known, as the better-informed did. The formal freedoms of democracy meant little, since they gave men and women rights they could not exercise. Collective judgments, arrived at by those who knew, would serve everyone best.

Despite the finicky distaste for popular culture and popular politics, intellectuals were ready to use and be used by the modern media. They owed it to the public to communicate through the "Today" show, or the book club, or the pages of *Playboy*. The few who became rich and famous often despised themselves, and those who failed tasted the gall of frustration.

Revisionist historiography added a dash of indignant justification to the anti-American brew by inventing grounds for the belief that the United States shared at least an equal portion of guilt for the cold war. Professor Gabriel Kolko argued that the Soviet Union had borne the brunt of World War II, while the United States contributed little to victory and only prepared to consume the spoils. Professor William Appleman Williams discerned a postwar plot to establish American hegemony over an exhausted world. These fantastic interpretations survived despite repeated demonstration that those who contrived them falsified the record and despite revelations year after year that showed the moral differences between the Soviet and Western regimes. Intellectuals clung to the faith in American culpability because it filled their need for reasons to hate their country and its democracy. Maybe, wrote a critic in *The New York Review of Books,* "the revisionist view can be sustained only by distorting the historical record. But maybe such distortions, even where they can be demonstrated, do not undercut the central revisionist argument about the origins of the cold war."

By the end of the 1970s the masochists within the government accepted the revisionist line and, in a delirium of self-persecution, readily concurred in the view of their country as a plunderer of poorer nations, a supporter of tyranny throughout the world, and a racist foe of human rights. President Carter early announced his intention to escape from the "inordinate fear of Communism"; and he brought into the upper echelons of his administration men and women of the new-line persuasion, some of them affiliated with the Institute for Policy Studies, a revisionist think tank. The Soviet invasion of Afghanistan forced the shocked president into a reappraisal, although the change of regime in Kabul a year earlier had been as significant as the act of aggression; however, the advisers responsible for the earlier Carter policy lingered in office. Ronald Reagan, the new president, elected in 1980, had reasons to brood about the means of restoring a more benign view of his country and its future.

The deeper roots of anti-Americanism lay in misanthropy. Brendan Behan once observed that whoever hated America hated mankind. Mark Twain articulated his bitterest emotions in criticisms of his country: "The red letter days of the calendar are April 1, which reminds us that we are fools and October 12, Columbus Day. It would have been wonderful to find America, but it would have been more wonderful to miss it." But then, in *Letters from the Earth*, he described man as the cruel animal, the only one that "deals in the atrocity of atrocities, WAR." He alone goes "forth in cold blood and with calm pulse to exterminate his kind."

In the writing of the 1970s, again and again, Americans in particular and people in general appeared as the despoilers — all their works a source of corruption and pollution. That society was a prison was the theme of many a novel; and the overpowering sense of revulsion extended to the imperfect world around it: "This earth, my home, a pint-sized pimple in a second-rate solar system stuck off in some miserable corner of the universe. It needs an enema. AN ENEMA. One last, great, screaming, suicidal douche until all the pressure blows off the poles and water gushes out of its navel." In *The Blue Lagoon* and *Urban Cowboy* hatred of civilization crept into the movies. The aversion to risk — the trepidation in the face of any alteration in forces deemed natural — accounted for the withdrawal from the exploration of outer space, from the supersonic-transport program, and from the development of nuclear energy. Slow economic growth, a falling birthrate, a decline in the rate of savings, and expansion of the nonproductive sector of the population were indexes of loss of faith in the future.

Hatred of humanity was thus the dominant tone of Howard Zinn's *A People's History of the United States* (1980), a book without merit except as a symptom of the prevailing ennui. No modern country received a favorable mention in this volume. It spoke well of the Russian and Chinese revolutions, but not of the states they created. It lavished indiscriminate condemnation upon civilization, a word it usually enclosed in quotation marks. Its heroes were not real people but idealized types who never existed.

The Arawaks were the subject of Zinn's *History*. Once upon a time, a folk remarkable for their belief in sharing and for their hospitality lived blissfully without commerce, for they relied exclusively upon the natural environment for sustenance. They valued the arts, and accorded freedom and dignity to both sexes. Ages before the Arawaks, the Mound Builders, also devoted to the arts, had occupied the same continent. And from across the ocean came black Africans out of such idyllic communal groups that they hardly needed law; and even slavery was benign. Then the destructive white strangers arrived — and it was downhill all the way.

Such was the story Zinn purported to unfold. Focusing upon the dimly known Arawaks of the past, whose shadowy shapes could take any form, the book could not do justice to the great variety of actual people who inhabited the United States. The blacks and whites, immigrants and natives, laborers and farmers, merchants and manufacturers could not be known when treated as lay figures to be manipulated according to the author's fantasies.

The intellectuals of earlier generations looked toward the future and had faith in man's works. Those of the 1970s unable to find hope in progress looked to the past — not to the immediate or known past, but to some distant, imagined era. They mourned the loss of innocence. As long as the

New World was an empty wilderness, they inscribed upon it all the images critical of their own society. They could no longer do so when an actual civilization, peopled by living men and women, occupied the formerly free space.

Against the civilization of his own time, Zinn's epilogue juxtaposed a loving community of neighbors who cooperated without coercion, a community exemplified by the Arawaks — fit objects for fantasy because nothing was known about them. Early on, Zinn, quoted a Spaniard's description of other preinvasion Indians who lived in peace and amity — six hundred in a conical hut. Life may have been carefree, even idyllic, but it could not have been easy under those circumstances. No doubt a twentieth-century American would find the actuality difficult to imagine — six hundred people to a hut. And perhaps the events in Jonestown showed what could happen to such numbers cooped up together, driven in upon one another in their loving community.

Few such societies were driven to suicide, as was that in Guyana. But rarely were any of them able to deal with the crises and contingencies of human experience.

And it is in that regard that Americans can learn something from the Arawaks, although Zinn was too obtuse to do so. What discussion ensued among those Indians who greeted Columbus or Cortes we shall never know. Perhaps they hoped by friendly gestures to propitiate the strangers and persuade them to leave. Perhaps, already conscious of their own helplessness, they thought to stave off attack by appeasement. Perhaps internal dissension, or lack of organization, or will weakened by ease prevented them from following another course. Without evidence, we cannot know. But the outcome we do know and from it we can learn. From Montezuma to Tecumseh, people who lacked the political means to defend themselves were helpless to resist the invading others animated by a vision of what they wanted and driven by the will to seize it.

The slide toward neutralism tempts those without taste for the dirty tools of power. Few Americans will go the whole way with the pacifist argument: let each country abjure the destructive weapons that crowd the arsenals of all; let each end suspicion and create understanding by dismantling its intelligence services and sending home its troops for constructive work. Experience warns of the consequences.

But not a few begin to wonder: What have we to do with events in Gdansk, or Basra, or other distant places? Perhaps Herbert Hoover was correct, after all, when he urged his countrymen to stay away from the sordid affairs of other peoples and withdraw to the security of Fortress America.

Alas, there is no security in the one world of the 1980s. Conceivably the United States could relieve itself of all dependence upon imported energy. It might forget that Third World debts soared from $75 billion in 1973 to $250 billion in 1980 and that a tide of petrodollars could inundate the world's banks. Perhaps the United States could somehow write off its overseas investments and disentangle its economy from that of its partners. It could compromise its claims to oceanic fisheries and underwater resources. It might be willing to accept lowered standards of living and pay the price of fading hopes of social advancement in the unrest that would follow. It could surrender its historic sense of mission and sever all cultural ties with the lands across the ocean. Yet its destiny would still be linked inextricably with theirs.

The world's problems mount at a staggering pace; and no social system other than the American has shown the capacity to cope with them. Today almost 60 percent of the world's population of 4.3 billion are poor. Twenty years from the date this page is written the total population of the world will have soared to 6 billion and the percentage of the poor will have risen, for they enjoy the highest birthrates. The 230 million Americans, whose numbers will have remained roughly stationary, will have to survive amidst peoples mired in poverty, their only assets massive numbers and massive arsenals. The situation of a world running down makes an unlovely subject for contemplation.

There is no turning back the clock of history. The dreams of the 1950s are gone without prospect for recovery. There are no means left to breathe life again into the concepts of collective security and international law.

Soviet clumsiness may yet give the free world a respite to discover equivalents. Communist society has not solved either its internal problems or its difficulties in dealing with other states — even with its ideological neighbors. Witness the events of 1980 in Poland and Afghanistan.

But proper employment of the interval demands abandonment of illusions and recognition of necessity, pursuit of the possible, not of the ultimately desirable. It requires also recognition by the free world of its own identity, of the absolute moral differences that separate it from the totalitarian regimes with which it shares the globe. And the time left will be wasted upon those who fail to understand that they inhabit one world with others and must summon up the will to defend values from the past that are still valid for the future.

Acknowledgments

WHILE I HAVE reconsidered afresh every statement in this volume in the light of events through 1980, some chapters draw upon essays written and published earlier. I am grateful to the editors of the journals in which those essays appeared for criticism and assistance in composition and for permission, where required, to reprint in this form. For the opinions expressed I am, of course, solely responsible.

Chapter 2 draws upon Oscar Handlin, *One World: The Origins of an American Concept. An Inaugural Lecture Delivered before the University of Oxford on 23 February 1973* (Oxford: Clarendon Press, 1974).

Chapter 3 originates in "The Failure of Communism — and What It Portends," *The Atlantic,* December 1961, pp. 40 ff.

Chapter 4 draws upon "The Gullibility of the Neutrals," *The Atlantic,* March 1963, pp. 41 ff.

I have treated some of the subjects of chapter 5 in "The Ethics of the Eichmann Case," *Issues* 15 (1961): 1 ff.; "Ethics and Eichmann," *Commentary* 30 (August 1960): 161 ff.; and "Hannah Arendt's Eichmann," *New Leader* 45 (5 August 1963): 19 ff.

Some aspects of the discussion in chapter 6 appeared in "Dissent, Democracy and Foreign Policy," Foreign Policy Association, *Headline Series,* no. 190 (August 1968). Some topics in chapter 7 were treated in "Solzhenitsyn Reconsidered," *Freedom at Issue,* no. 52 (September 1979), pp. 17 ff.; and "Comments," *Commentary* 49 (January 1980): 39 ff. Solzhenitsyn's address appears in Aleksandr I. Solzhenitsyn, *A World Split Apart* (New York: Harper & Row, 1978); and Ronald Berman, ed., *Solzhenitsyn at Harvard* (Washington: Ethics & Public Policy Center, 1980).

Some subjects in chapter 8 received more extended treatment in "Does the People's Rule Doom Democracy?" *Commentary* 20 (November 1955): 1 ff.; "Liberal Democracy and the Image of America," in *A Prospect of Liberal Democracy,* ed. William S. Livingston (Austin: U. of Texas Press, 1979), pp. 43 ff.; and "Arawaks," *American Scholar,* 49 (Autumn 1980): 546 ff.

I am grateful to John Pippa for help in preparing the manuscript. I owe much to Laura Margolis for efficiency and good nature in freeing my time and organizing my work on this book.

I owe much also to the learning and good sense of Lilian Handlin.

— O. H.